Reviewers and Financial Professionals say...

"The key strength of the volume is its simple system for record organization... those who follow Peterson's hints could significantly reduce their expenses." *Publishers Weekly*

"This lively, common sense guide... is well organized... a simple and practical system." *Copley News Service*

"One of the better books of its kind that I have ever read. Peterson inspires me. Thrifty, orderly fun!" *Baltimore Sun*

"Jean Peterson really shows us how to 'Turn Chaos Into Cash.' " *Los Angeles Herald Examiner*

"...text starts from the ground up... basic information on investments, debts, credit... simple language for the unorganized." *Booklist*

"Your book has become the 'textbook' for my clients: typical two income couples, overextended on credit cards, records in complete disarray, unaware of how to save money. Your system implants good habits early and helps me to establish a planner/client relationship for a lifetime." *J.R. Cox, Blankinship & Associates, Financial Planning Advisers*

"I have found this book to be an excellent tool in helping my clients get their act together. Your common sense ideas, and the practical and unintimidating way they are presented, make it almost easy for people who find financial planning an unimpenetrable fog, to find their way. I absolutely recommend this book as a vital step to achieving financial independence." *M.W. Hoover, V.P., E.F. Hutton*

"After years of mishandling my financial records... and three IRS audits, I have finally found a system that really works. Thanks to Jean Ross Peterson's *Organize Your Personal Finances, Turn Chaos Into Cash*, I am now putting both my personal money matters and my business expense records in good order. No question about it: Peterson's book has saved me time... and money. I recommend it highly." *Robert Carter, Marketing Consultant, Editor, Trade Book Marketing, New York, N.Y.*

Organize Your Personal Finances

Organize Your Personal Finances

TURN CHAOS INTO CASH

Jean Ross Peterson

bp

BETTERWAY PUBLICATIONS, Incorporated
White Hall, Virginia

Published by Betterway Publications, Inc.
White hall, VA 22987

Cover design by Diane Nelson
Typography by East Coast Typography, Inc.

Library of Congress Cataloging in Publication Data

Peterson, Jean Ross
    Organize your personal finances.

    Includes index.
    1. Finance, Personal.   I. Title.
HG179.P445 1984   332.024   84-12293
ISBN 0-932620-36-1 (pbk.)

Printed in the United States of America
09876543

For Lee
Daughter, Friend, Mentor

Acknowledgements

I feel deep gratitude to these friends for their participation in this book. Their contributions span years and are both subtle and specific.

Helen Ross, Charles Ross, May Ruth Seidel, Don Waldemer, Mary Ann Daily, George Jedenoff, Martha Waddell, Karen Brownstein, Chester Johnson, and my companions at the Santa Barbara Writers Conference.

Contents

Author's Note

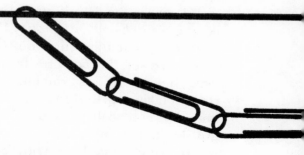

Some years ago, as I prepared my lecture, *How To Organize Your Personal Finances,* I wondered about the people who would be sitting in the classroom. The class was scheduled for Wednesday nights, from seven until ten o'clock. It was the first time the college had offered this course, so there was no precedent to help me anticipate who would enroll in the lecture series.

Will they be city residents or suburbanites? I asked myself. Am I going to see jeans and jogging shoes or three piece suits and briefcases? What are their financial and educational backgrounds and experiences? Will there be young singles, retirees, widows, middle aged couples — who *are* the people who want to learn how to manage their money?

Today, many classes and private client consultations later, I am still ignorant of the distinct answers to these questions because each possible answer has proven to be a correct one. While the composition of the classes includes almost every imaginable description of an individual from our adult population, the dialogues that take place in these classes remain consistent and predictable.

"We don't want generalities; we want specifics. Please keep it simple and don't quote statistics; we want practical information. Everyone knows records are important — we want to know *which* records to keep, *where* to find information, and *how* to put it all together."

However, this book is more than practical answers to precise questions. It includes a philosophy of money. I admit it is my personal philosophy and my enthusiasm for it approaches that of a zealot's. (No doubt you will soon realize that I hope to convert you.) What is the philosophy? I call it the *paper clip philosophy of finance* and you will find it scattered throughout the pages in the book. Simplistically stated, this is the definition: *Luxuries and a secure retirement are purchased with money NOT spent on paper clips.*

At this point I am sure you will ask yourself, does the person writing this book really believe that by finding and using free paper clips I can buy one hundred shares of IBM stock or take a trip to Hong Kong? No, of course I don't and I know you don't believe it either. Neither of us is ignorant nor gullible. On the other hand . . . many of my investments and my luxuries are purchased with "free paper clips." There are additional ways to express this philosophy. It is the value of dollars withheld from spending. It is the conservation of capital. It is limiting the abuse of obtaining necessities in order to enjoy luxuries.

Is this philosophy applicable and appropriate in our society today? Are computers and paper clips compatible? I am convinced they are. Furthermore, I am certain they are essential components! The "paper clip" finances of every individual, family, corporation and government are still the determining factor in the "win or lose," "succeed or fail" situation.

Frequently we hear the axiom, "money can't buy happiness." I respond to that statement by asking you to define happiness. Each of us has a different answer. If you are ill, money can't buy a miracle cure but it will provide the finest medical care available. Money can't reconcile a broken marriage, but it will hire a lawyer and support a family. The pains of loneliness, unemployment, old age, unfulfilled dreams and aspirations — all the realities and inherent heartaches of life are eased and gentled with money. Perhaps it is arrogant and privileged to say money doesn't buy happiness.

To illustrate both the philosophy of money and the organization of money, I have used examples from actual situations in my life, in the lives of people I know, or from the experiences of my private clients. I have not fabricated or imagined any part of the book in order to support my statements. The practical system I describe for the organization of personal finances is one I have developed and used during my lifetime. The tangible success of this system is evident in many lives; mine, friends, clients, and the men and women who attend my classes.

If my words could bludgeon you into establishing this system for financial organization, maintaining the system, and achieving your success, I would not hesitate to use them in that way. As an alternative, I beg, plead, and cajole you to organize your way to your happiness.

1.

Money: Not Finance

Do you wonder what's happening to your money? Have you ever said, "My finances are a mess?"

This book is written for you.

I will teach you — in the same way I teach the men and women who attend my classes — how to take care of your money. You will learn an easy, step-by-step method, one you can use now and in all the years ahead, for the organization of every part of your financial life. *More* money is the unpreventable by-product of this process.

Somerset Maugham said, "Money is like a sixth sense, and you can't enjoy the other five without it." I agree, but will add — "and you can't enjoy money if you worry about it."

Dollars and sense

How you earn your money is up to you. There probably is as much advice on how and where to invest, as there is money to be invested. My goal is to show you how to put an end to your worry about money so you can enjoy it.

Your living requires money; so does your dying. It's what gets you places, as in cars, busses, and airplanes. You put it in parking meters, rush to deposit it on payday, and hand it to the checker at the supermarket. Money should not be confused with finance.

Finance is precious metals, partnerships, and tax shelters. The only shelter most of us will have is the one we call home. The partnerships we will look for are the ones for the card table and the tennis court. When I use the words financial or finance, I'm talking about money!

[15]

Become your own money manager

You *must* become your own money manager. The harsh reality is, nobody (not even I) really cares about your money the way you do . . . or should. I care about mine.

Money management — the worry-free system I explain in the following chapters — will never be carefree. I make that distinction because the care of money, the way you use your dollars, is always changing. There will be changes in how you earn, save, spend, and invest as long as you live.

On the other hand, a system to free you from the worry and chaos of money management is possible. It also can be flexible enough to see you through all the changes in your financial situations.

In addition, a worry-free and flexible system will give you the time you need for intelligent evaluation of the financial changes that take place in our economy and in the economies of the rest of the world. Laws affecting money will change. The value of money will change. There always will be some change in money!

By the time you finish this book, you will be your own money manager. You will have confidence in yourself, and I do care about that — a lot! Never again will you want somebody else to be your financial dictator. From that point on, you will ask the questions, evaluate the answers, and then make your own decisions. Money is a pleasure. Managing your own money is a great pleasure. It's not complicated or confusing. Everyone can do it.

There are two requirements for becoming your own money manager. One is to want to do it. The other is to know how to do it. You decide on the first requirement; I'll take care of the second one.

The paper chase

Just as money is always full of change, it also always includes paper. Not paper dollars, but all the thousands of pieces of paper that are created by the ways you use your dollars. Those pieces of paper can drive you crazy! So this also is a book about paper and what to do with it.

Our lives are filled with paper, our time consumed by it, our actions controlled by it, our living recorded on it. We begin our paper collection on the day we are born — with a birth certificate. We can't even die without one last piece of paper — a death certificate. True, some of our paper past can be thrown away, but we must save much of it for our paper future. Our paper present must be preserved.

As you read through this book, you will learn how to have comprehensive records for every paper transaction in your financial life. You will have a place, one that makes sense to you now and in all the years ahead, for all those troublesome but necessary pieces of paper. You can throw away your shoebox!

Prove your point

Life today is complex; often chaotic. This is particularly true of our financial life. The once simple tasks of depositing money in a bank and writing a check have become complicated with choices that require our thoughtful and informed judgment. As our personal finances become more and more involved with computers, it is imperative to develop and *maintain* our own system of organization and record keeping for our dollars and financial activities. We must have a way to talk back to the computers and we must be able to do it with authority — the authority of printed proof to support and validate our actions.

My ideas on the need for printed proof are not new. The *Apocrypha* in the *Book of Ecclesiasticus* admonishes, "When you make a deposit, see that it is counted and weighed, and when you give or receive, have it in writing." Some things don't change.

Record keeping must be both uncomplicated and infallible if we are to avoid both chaos and excessive demands on our time. I don't want to spend more than ten minutes finding the paper proof of one of my financial transactions that took place eight years ago. If the organization of personal finances is cumbersome and time consuming, there is every possibility — probability — that the tasks will be avoided. We will, by default, succumb to the anxiety of ignorance about our own money. Furthermore, we will let some other person or machine govern all that we work for and strive to accomplish.

The "insiders' " vocabulary

In the business of money, as in the business of sports, gambling, law, sewage disposal, etc., there is a special "insiders' " vocabulary. If the words used in any particular business are understood only by those in the business, then they, the "insiders," can call themselves experts. In our society we have come to equate *exclusive* with *better*. Perhaps, even with best. I don't buy that! Exclusive words don't create experts. Let me show you what I mean by "insiders' " vocabulary. I'll pick some words from the business of money.

Cash flow. Entire seminars and book chapters are devoted to cash flow. What is it? It's how much money you have coming in and how much money you have going out. A child can understand those words. But to be an expert you must say "cash flow."

I often wonder about the person who decided cash would flow. To flow means to glide, to proceed smoothly and evenly. Have you ever seen cash do that? Not I! My cash comes in slowly, in uneven amounts and at irregular times. It fairly leaps away from me as if it had a propulsive energy all its own. Anyone who would combine cash and flow can't, it seems to me, have had much experience with either word.

Personal balance sheet — more of the favorite words used by the experts who advise about money. Have you ever looked at an example of a personal balance sheet? I suggest you do and look at the items listed under assets: hobbies, furs, boats, vacation home, furniture. These are typical items you are to include in your *net worth* (there's another of those "insiders' " expressions). Well really! Does anyone think I am so ignorant that I will believe my old fur coat can do anything but feed moths? My furniture is an asset in that I can sit on it. My vacation home is folded up in my garage along with my camp stove and sleeping bag. My hobbies include a rusty rake and shovel, hiking boots, and pictures of my vacations. *Net worth*? Who do they think they're kidding!

When I teach about money I use "real" words and I avoid the ones from the "insiders' " vocabulary. I could call teaching a class, "presenting a seminar." I won't. Similarly, the words in this book are the plain, simple words for financial organization. I will convince you that you are the expert in the management of your money. It is actions, not words, that create experts.

Trust your instincts

I always am gratified to find substantiation for my opinions in similar ideas expressed by someone else — particularly someone who has received recognition and distinction by evidential accomplishments. Ellen Goodman, Pulitzer Prize winning columnist, recently wrote, "We seem to belong to a culture that trusts its experts more than its instincts."

While I have quoted her words out of context, the message is clear. Too many of us refuse to believe in ourselves and in our own ability to choose the expert actions for ourselves. As an illustration, which of these choices would you make?

Would you have a successful, experienced lawyer help you organize your finances, or would you prefer to do it yourself? If you chose the lawyer, you could be in trouble.

I recently spent an hour in a lawyer's office. The attorney was both amazed and intrigued by my financial records. Every one of his questions was answered immediately with my printed facts and figures. As we left his conference room, the lawyer said, "I wish you'd help me get my finances organized. They're in a terrible mess."

Moreover, in whom do you have greater confidence for the management of your money — you, or a wealthy businessman who graduated from one of the three top-ranking business schools in the United States? If you chose the man with the business degree, you might yet have problems. This man came to me for help in setting up a system for his investment records (I found it hard to believe, too!). His business vocabulary was flawless. The only ingredient missing was . . . common sense.

Education, wealth, sex, profession — none of these are the guarantees of, or the requirements for, expertise. Many of the experts saying *cash flow* and *personal balance sheet* have their own finances in muddled disarray.

We are almost ready to make order out of chaos (unless, of course, you have decided you don't want to, in which case I'll say goodbye to you now). For those of you who decided to take control of your dollars, stay with me here for another minute or two . . . then I'll help you get organized.

I want to ask you one more question before we get going on your shoe box mess. What is money? You'd be surprised at some of the answers I get from the men and women who attend my classes. Here is the way I think about money. I wish you'd try it.

Money is interest

Mathematically, ten $10.00 bills and ten percent of one thousand dollars are the same amount. $100.00. Philosophically and psychologically they are not at all equal. They are very different amounts of money. How can that be true?

It isn't hard to remove a ten dollar bill from your billfold to pay for a couple of movie tickets. Take out another ten dollars and buy a wrench, subscribe to a magazine, and so on. Soon you have painlessly, perhaps more or less thoughtlessly, given away one hundred dollars.

However, take one thousand dollars out of your income. Put it away someplace for an entire year where it will earn you ten percent interest. Now try to spend *that* one hundred dollars — the interest from the thousand you invested. You will find you use your interest money a lot differently than you used those ten $10.00 bills in your billfold. A new sense of the value of money emerges. You will have greater discrimination in how you use your money.

When you think of money, think of it as interest. Don't see it as dollar bills. Two movie tickets cost 10% of $100.00 —after you have waited one year for your money to earn the admission price for you. It's not easy to find a movie worth that much money. Money is interest!

Now that you know what it is, it's time to organize it. Once you establish this system of organization, it will take you about twenty minutes a week to maintain it. Seventeen hours a year yield peace of mind and financial control. Not a bad return on an investment!

2.

Organize — Don't Agonize

I'll be honest. Record keeping is not glamorous. At first only your bank balance will benefit; not your ego.

If you go to a party and mention you bought XYZ stock at 8 and it's now trading at 37, you'll get lots of attention. People will crowd around and ask you questions. They will want your advice. You'll feel terrific.

On the other hand, should you announce, "I keep excellent records. I am extremely well organized." Well, I hope you like to drink alone and talk to yourself.

Eventually your ego will benefit when you take a vacation, buy a new tennis racket, pay a child's school tuition, donate to your favorite charity, or pick out a new car. Indeed, you will be able to give the greatest of all gifts to yourself and to your family — your financial independence. You won't worry about your money. The people who love you won't worry about your financial future. They would rather give you love than money anyway.

You're going to read a few ideas in this book and say to yourself, "Everyone knows that. I've been doing that for years."

Maybe you have, but you would be surprised at the number of people who don't know, and who don't do, those things you consider obvious and elementary. Finding a few familiar ideas and suggestions should confirm for you that you are doing some things the right way.

Experience has taught me never to make an assumption. I would rather include the obvious, than to have one reader miss the information.

If you were worth several million dollars, would you have a will? I am aware of one man who does not.

If you had your own business, would you know how much money you have in the bank? I know a woman who doesn't have any idea what her bank balance is.

Could you believe a doctor must borrow money for his son's college tuition? I know one who does, year after year, because he spends all his money before he actually earns it.

How about a bright young woman, with a college degree, who can't figure out what credit cards she needs, or how to go about getting them.

These are real people, in very real situations. Is it any wonder I make no assumptions as to who does what with personal finances?

Piggy banks

Let's get started. The first step is into a bank. The first lesson is: all banks are *piggy banks*. To be "piggy" is to be greedy — to keep mine and get yours, too. I am not criticizing banks for being piggy banks but you should know they are. They are in business to make money and if they don't, they fail. Lately some of them have.

In addition to not giving anything away, such as bank services, it's good to know that nobody decided to become a banker because it was the best way to find friends. I don't care if my friendly banker calls me Jean, customer, or account number 321. I do care what I am charged for banking services, the interest I get on my deposits, and the interest I have to pay for a loan. I shop for a bank the way I shop for anything else — to get the most value in return for the fewest dollars. And I always am skeptical of advertising and promotions that promise something in return for nothing.

Put your banker — one of the professionals you hire to work for you — on your support team. Other members of your support team include your doctor, lawyer, tax advisors, broker, etc. Without you and me and all the rest of us, these professionals would not have jobs. We pay their salaries. At a bank you are buying a service, not a friend.

Checks and checkbooks

Obviously, the first service you need at your bank is a checking account. Costs for this usually depend on how many checks you write in a month and how much money you keep in the bank. Figure out what kind of a checking account is best suited to your needs. Talk to your banker.

Equally apparent, to use a checking account, you need checks and a checkbook. I prefer the large binder size checkbook called a desk type, or executive style. In spite of the name, executive style, I use this kind of checkbook because it allows me the space I need for my record keeping. Many people say at this point, "But I have to carry my checkbook with me." No you don't! You have credit cards and you use them wisely (I'll say more about that later). You have a limited amount of cash for your small purchases such as greeting cards, bus fares, lunches, and parking charges. I carry one, and only one, blank check with me. That one blank check is for an emergency. The same check usually stays in my billfold an entire year. A checkbook in your pocket or purse encourages impulse spending. You can't buy it if you can't pay for it.

Once you have chosen your bank and selected your account and your checkbook, then you have to decide what you want printed on your checks. You should include your name and your address but nothing more. Don't add your telephone number, social security number, driver's license number, etc. I realize someone can find your telephone number once your name and address is known, but why make it easy? Some of the scoundrels in this world are lazy! Keep your private life as private as possible even though it is becoming increasingly difficult to do so. You can always write in your telephone number if it is required.

Your new checkbook and checks are sent to you . . . now it's time to pay your bills.

Writing checks and paying bills

The easiest way to learn how to write checks (and many people don't know how) is to imagine yourself sitting at your desk or table. In front of you is your pile of bills and your new checkbook. First go through your bills and see when each one is due. The 5th, 15th, and so on. Now put the bills in a new pile in the same order in which they are due. Let's assume it is the 2nd of the month when you do this. You probably have only a few bills due on the 5th. Those are the ones you will pay now. The rest don't get paid until a couple of days before they are due. Do not give anyone your money until you have to! As long as you have it, it's earning interest income for you.

Now let's say the first bill in your "pay now" pile is from an insurance agency. In addition to the date, amount, and the name of the person or company to whom you are writing a check, there is more information to be written on a check. And on the check stub. On this first check you are writing —remember it's for insurance — you will include the number of your insurance policy. There usually is a blank space somewhere at the bottom of the check, opposite the line for your signature. If this bill is for one half a year's premium, then write, "6 months premium." Write "annual premium" if you are paying for a whole year's coverage.

The policy number and period covered by this payment also are written on your check stub. If this insurance is for health, add the letter "D" to the bottom, left hand corner of your check stub. Why? "D" is for deduct. Health insurance costs, at least at the time I am writing, can still count toward your medical deductions on your income taxes.

The letter "D" goes on a check stub every time you write a check to a charity, non-profit organization, religious group, for energy saving equipment, a safe deposit box, papers and books (this one!) on financial advice, alimony, glasses — you see the point. All checks for things affecting your taxes get the big "D". You don't want one honest deduction to escape you when it is time to pay those taxes.

The numbers game

To continue with the suggestions for information you include on your checks as you write them . . . a check to the telephone company gets your telephone number. A check for auto registration gets your license number. A check for taxes gets your social security number. In other words, add on all your appropriate identifying numbers. Your numbers are as important as your name these days — perhaps more important.

In addition to the numbers that identify you, it is advisable to include the numbers that specify the purpose of your payments. For example, suppose you are writing a check for a newspaper subscription. Does the person receiving your money know if you are a new subscriber or is this a renewal? What is the time period covered by your payment? Is it for three months beginning in June, or is it for two months beginning in July? Why should you include so much additional information on your checks? Because the person who opens your envelopes and handles your payments is human. That person has all the problems and distractions available to all of us. Perhaps she has a sick child at home. Maybe his girl friend walked out on him. In either case, crediting customers' accounts is not the most exciting job in the world and any distraction can lead to errors. It takes so little time and effort on your part to insure that your checks pay for goods and services in compliance with your intent.

Back to paying the bills. You have written the check, added on all the information to help you maintain your record keeping, put the same information on the check stub, and now you are ready to put the check in an envelope. Wait! You forgot to sign the check. Do you know your name? That's a not-so-silly question.

What's in a name?

Decide on your name now — the one form of your name you will use for everything in your financial and legal life and then never change that name. Women often change the last part of their names if they marry but today many women are choosing to keep their original names for financial, professional, and legal purposes.

Here is a personal example of what I mean about the form of a name. I am Jean Ross Peterson. I am not J. Ross Peterson nor am I, J. R. Peterson. Jean Ross Peterson is the name on my credit cards, bank accounts, will, library card, this book, passport, and the aluminum ladder I lend to my neighbors.

You may wonder why I make such an issue out of the name you use. Computers can't read handwriting and they are infantile in their deductive reasoning capability. They have no way of knowing that J. R. Peterson is Jean Ross Peterson. Haven't we all received duplicate mailings in which only the form of our name is different? Computers need help if they are going to know who paid a bill or made a bank deposit. *Now* sign your check.

You probably have a part of the bill or statement from the insurance company they want returned to them. Do it. Help the computers again. The other part of the bill, sometimes marked "customer's copy" is the part you get to keep. It's one of the pieces of paper you used to throw in a show box. No longer. On this piece of paper, your copy of the bill, write the number of the check you just wrote to the insurance company and the date on which you wrote it. Check number 101; 5/2/85.

Put this customer's copy in a pile, someplace where it won't get lost or thrown away. Later on you're going to put it in the file I will help you set up in the following chapter. Don't panic. The file is easy to do. I can file all my pieces of paper from a whole month in about twenty minutes.

At this point, you have become an expert at writing checks and paying bills. It is shocking how few people know the correct way to perform this routine, basic activity. Actually, you have done more than that. You have begun an important part of your new money management process.

I would like to pick a word, now, to describe this money management process. I choose *system*. It is simple and short. I'll use it from here on.

Keeping your balance

You cannot write checks (or you should not) unless you have money in the bank. You must know how much money you have in the bank at all times. Balance your checkbook as you go along. This is sometimes called "keeping a running balance." That doesn't mean your money is running away from you. It means you subtract each check *as you write it* from the previous total in your checkbook.

Let's look on the bright side. Not all your money has gone away. Some has come in. (Remember *cash flow?*) Your bank sent you deposit slips when they sent your checks. They know you need income to pay those bills. For a welcome change from bill paying, let's discuss some of the income checks you might have.

Proof of deposit

One is your salary check, one is $10.00 from your uncle on your birthday, one is $18.72 interest on money you have invested in your cash emergency fund or "safety account". (I will explain this "safety account" in the next chapter.) Don't forget the words from the *Apocrypha* "always get a receipt for a deposit". My bank doesn't issue deposit forms with carbon copies for the customer so I must always request a written receipt from the teller. It is a nuisance but I always do it. Come the day the computer and I have an argument over my deposit, I don't want the computer to win.

No doubt you have realized by now I bank in person and not by mail. Careful reader that you are, you also have figured out I do not use the "automatic tellers" and the bank's secret code card. You bet I don't!

Bank by mail

A deposit by mail spends two or more days getting to the bank and those are days during which I am losing interest (my money — not my attention). Those also can be days the post office spends losing my deposit checks.

Depositing income checks in person is not a hard and fast rule. There are exceptions.

Limitations on personal mobility (lack of transportation, poor health) may make it hard for you to get to a bank. If you travel for business or pleasure and are frequently out of town, your income checks will reach the bank faster if they are sent by the issuer directly to your account. A direct deposit by mail of regular income checks (social security, interest, dividends, etc.) is the best way to have these dollars working for you under the circumstances I have mentioned. Your responsibility is careful scrutiny of your bank statements to verify the deposits. Watch for both the amount and the date of all direct mail deposits to your account. You can never afford to relax your vigilance over the actions of other people (or machines) who handle your money.

Automatic tellers

As for the banking machines . . . I don't like them. I have read stories about mistakes these machines make. I have heard about situations where secret code cards are not so secret anymore. Banks "tell" me I can't live without one of their secret code cards. I am told I will need money for an emergency. Of course they don't know I am well organized. They forgot they issued me a credit card to take care of emergencies. I get my cash for the weekend, and the following week, on Friday when banks stay open late. Or I do my banking on my lunch hour.

A "glitch"

What might happen to you if you rely upon an automatic teller? Here is an actual situation that took place in one of the major cities in the United States. It was reported in a Tuesday morning newspaper, following a three-day national holiday.

The vice-president of one of the largest banks in America apologized to all the customers who tried to use their plastic cards at the banks' machines over the three-day holiday weekend and found they, the customers, couldn't get any money. Why did the machines, the automatic tellers, refuse to let the customers have their money? Because the machines had run out of money! Someone had forgotten to supply the machines with all the cash necessary to provide the customers with their emergency funds. The vice-president went on to say that the situation was not intentional. I should hope not! That excuse, or apology, did not help the person who needed cash to pay for the activities scheduled during the three-day holiday. He also explained that some of the machines failed to deliver the promised money because of a computer "glitch".

The word "glitch" is one we will hear and see with increasing frequency. I looked it up in a dictionary and this is the definition I found. "A sudden malfunction of equipment or of a plan or scheme." My life is complicated as it is; I do not intend to add a *glitch* or seek a *scheme* if I can avoid one.

My decision to bank in person is the one I have made based on my own careful judgment of the choices available to me. I'm not telling you to do it my way. I am saying why I bank in person. If you do use the "automatic tellers," indicate cash withdrawals on your check stubs with an "X" (express stop) and file the machine receipt with cancelled checks.

Reflecting authority

Time out from banking. That last paragraph reminds me of something I want to be sure to comment on in this book. Right now seems a good time to say it.

I have been telling you to "do this" and "do that." Those are ideas and suggestions. They are not absolutes! I have had a lot of experience with the organizational methods I teach, both in classrooms and in private consultations. I use this system myself. However, you might figure out a better way to do something. Your situation could require changes in some phase of this system. Fine. Do it the way that is best for you. Use my advice as a guide for financial organization but never think someone else knows more about your money, and the care of your money, than you do. And that includes me!

With that out of the way, we can return to banking and put some money in your checking account. We were looking at some of your income checks and discussing your deposit slips.

Identifying income

Most deposit forms require a separate listing of each check, as well as the total amount of the deposit. On your deposit receipt write in the source of each check — where it came from, how you came to have it. It's not enough to know you deposited $10.00; you need to know your uncle sent it for your birthday.

In other words, you are identifying all your income. If one of your checks is a dividend, include the information "XYZ Company" on your deposit receipt. Make income tax preparation simple.

Reading your stubs

Each time you have a receipt for a deposit, staple it to one of your check stubs. Not to just any old stub. The receipt should be stapled to the check stub where you actually write in the amount of the deposit. (You may find it helpful to use a pen of a different color when you enter deposits.) To put it another way: wherever you add the deposit to your checking account balance in your checkbook, that's the same place, the very stub, to which you staple the receipt.

Just as you can read through your stubs, from one to the next, and see where your dollars went, you can also read the deposit receipts in the same way and identify all your income. This written record of dollars in and dollars out is invaluable to you — the expert money manager.

Make a statement

Once a month the bank sends you a statement and returns all your checks that have cleared through your account for the month. Compare their records with yours and be sure you agree with them as to how much money you have in the bank. If you don't know how to balance your checkbook (reconcile your balance with the bank's statement), ask a friend to help you. Or go to the bank and ask someone there to show you how to do it. Help the bankers earn their salaries.

Perhaps there is a mistake in your statement. Sometimes it is the bank that made the mistake — not you. I recently found a large deposit credited to my account that someone else had mailed to the bank. It took me time and effort to convince the bank it was not my money. After all, a machine had made the mistake and machines don't do such terrible things.

Keeping track

Along with your bank statement, you get back all those checks you wrote. Or almost all. Sometimes there are a few that haven't been cashed yet and they are "outstanding." They'll probably come back the next month. Anyway, for the checks that do come back, put a mark "✔" by the corresponding number on your check stub. For the checks that do not come back (clear), put a circle around the number on your check stub. The following month when the checks are returned, you can add a check mark to the circle and you never will lose track of your checks. You always will know which ones have been cashed and which ones are still sitting on some desk or (and it happens) are lost.

In the business of education, the experts are always talking about visual aids. That means, I have something to show you. The illustration on page 32 is a visual aid for the checkbook part of your system. You can see where I put a D. (check #101). I've written in the deposit information and shown you where to staple your deposit receipt. Check #102 is an example of a check that did not clear one month (102), but then came back the next month (102).

I just made up the numbers for my visual aid. I don't really know what a lamp costs; I haven't shopped for one in a long time. I have a lamp and I hate to buy anything I don't need. I put in this example in case you want to look over my shoulder to see how I do it. You'll find out, in Chapter Four, why there is a ✔ on the lower, left corner of each check.

Supplies

Where do you keep these bank statements and cancelled checks once you have reconciled the statement and marked off the check stubs in your checkbook? Buy a small 5 x 11 stiff paper file. These files are sold at stationery or business supply stores and are sometimes called accordion files even though the only sound they produce is your contented humming as you sense the rewards your new system will provide. They usually have a band attached to them so you can keep the file closed. Mine cost me fifty cents but I bought it years ago. It probably is $1.50 by now. Keep the cash register receipt from this file purchase. It's a tax deductible item. It is also one of the pieces of paper you must fit into your system. I have finished describing how to take care of checks, bills, bank statements (do I hear a sigh of relief?), but I still have not told you what to do with all the piles of paid bills and pieces of paper you've been accumulating. In the next chapter I will.

CHECKBOOK EXAMPLE

1. _____

Note:

1. Identification numbers on checks and stubs.
2. Income identification.
3. "Running balance".
4. "D": for all deductibles.
5. Tick mark ($\checkmark$) for notebook entries.

4. _____

2. _____

5. _____

3. _____

101 ✔ Balance Brought Forward	869 70
_____ 19_____	
PAY TO *My Health Insurance Co.*	
FOR *6 mos premium- Jan-June*	
DEPOSIT _____	
DEPOSIT _____ *Policy #* BALANCE	869 70
AMOUNT THIS CHECK	432 00
D ✔ BALANCE	437 70
(staple deposit receipt here) 102 ✔	437 70
_____ 19_____	
PAY TO *Telephone Co.*	
FOR *Jan.*	
DEPOSIT *10.00- uncle birthday*	687.50
DEPOSIT *658.78-salary* *18.72- interest on safety fund* BALANCE	1125 20
AMOUNT THIS CHECK	16 72
✔ BALANCE	1108 48
103 ✔	1108 48
_____ 19_____	
PAY TO *Department Store*	
FOR *lamp*	
DEPOSIT _____	
DEPOSIT _____ BALANCE	1108 48
AMOUNT THIS CHECK	47 80
✔ BALANCE	1060 68

NAME

ADDRESS

101

——————— 19 ——

Pay to the
order of _____ My Health Insurance Company _____ $ 432.<u>00</u> ^{no}

Four hundred thirty two and------------------------no/100 **Dollars**

policy number
For _____ 6 months premium _____ Signature

NAME

ADDRESS

102

——————— 19 ——

Pay to the
order of _____ Telephone Company _____ $ 16.<u>00</u> ⁷²

Sixteen and---72/100 **Dollars**

For _____ telephone number _____ Signature

NAME

ADDRESS

103

——————— 19 ——

Pay to the
order of _____ Department Store _____ $ 47.<u>00</u> ⁸⁰

Forty seven and-------------------------------------80/100 **Dollars**

For _____ account number _____ Signature

3.

Pieces of Paper

When you buy your small file for the statements and cancelled checks, buy a large 10 x 12 file at the same time. The small one has only one open space or "pocket." The big one (some people use the term "expanding file") has many of these file pockets. You will need a file with about 20 pockets in it. They often have alphabet letters at the top of each pocket, but that is not important. You are not going to need those letters anyway. I am appalled at the cost — about $7.00! But . . . it is tax deductible.

File labels

When you get home with your new file, you will need some labels to stick onto the top of each pocket. You can buy gummed labels but I get mine free (this is another example of my "paper clip philosophy"). I use name tags that were left over from a meeting or party. Most people buy more of these than they need and I ask if I can have the ones that were not used. You need only 20; it's a shame to pay for them.

Make one label for each of the following words or categories.

1. Auto/Transportation
2. Clothing
3. Deductibles
4. Insurance
5. Investments
6. Legal
7. Medical/Dental
8. Pleasure

9. Taxes
10. Shelter
11. Utilities
12. Income
13. Warranties/Guarantees
14. Personal
15. Professional, non-deductible
16. Inventory/Photos
17. Credit cards
18. Credit card purchase statements

Now stick the labels on the top of the pockets and get ready to file all those receipts — the pieces of paper. You don't have to be neat. Just toss them in the right pockets. Here are some suggestions for what papers go in which pockets.

1. **Auto/Transportation:** tires, gas, service fees, AAA dues, train tickets, bus passes, repairs, copy of auto insurance, auto insurance receipts, license fee, registration, violations.

2. **Clothing:** cleaning, alterations, new purchases.

3. **Deductibles:** gifts to non-profit groups, tax preparation, financial advice, job-related expenses, energy saving equipment.

4. **Insurance:** all insurance costs — except automobile.

5. **Investments:** records of all transactions for this year.

6. **Legal:** charges for preparation of documents, will, advice.

7. **Medical/Dental:** receipts for prescription drugs, glasses, bills, transportation expenses.

8. **Pleasure:** flowers, wine, movies, hobbies, records, pets, sports, leisure activities, magazine subscriptions, books, vacations, gifts (non-deductible).

9. **Taxes:** local, state, federal, property.

10. **Shelter:** everything for residence and property, except utilities.

11. **Utilities:** gas, oil, electric, water, telephone.

12. **Income:** all sources of income.

13. **Warranties/Guarantees:** all (except for automobile and related parts and equipment), date and place of purchase, maintenance instructions.

14. **Personal:** copies of vital certificates, resumé, health records (shots, operations, etc.).

15. **Professional, non-deductible:** gifts, entertainment, memberships.

16. **Inventory/Photos:** list of acquisitions, appraisals, photos, certificates of antiquity.

17. **Credit cards:** card numbers, how to report lost or stolen cards.

18. **Credit card purchase statements:** Visa bills, Mastercharge bills, department store bills. These statements include a variety of goods and services. The individual items will be separated into appropriate and specific categories when they are recorded in the notebook that is described in the next chapter.

As you look at my list of categories for the file pockets, you will notice I have suggested eighteen, but told you to have twenty labels. That's not a mistake. I'm sure you will want one or two divisions in your file I have not included. You might own rental property; the records for the current year would be kept in the file. Or you may own a condo in a ski resort, be on the board of a volunteer agency, have a small, part-time business — any of these activities will require records that belong in separate pockets.

Perfect timing

When you set up your file, don't try to have too many small, specific categories. You can waste a lot of time trying to figure out which piece of paper, which record and receipt, belongs in what file pocket. The categories I suggest represent a general breakdown of a typical personal financial situation. The objective of this system is to have a place for everything, without getting bogged down in tedious, time consuming "busy work."

I do my filing once a week. Some people do it every time they pay a bill. I wouldn't let more than a month go by without filing all the pieces of paper since the task seems too big then and you might put it off, or not do it at all.

A word of warning. If the pocket marked "pleasure" is becoming too full, you are doing something wrong. The problem is not in the system. I'll be saying more about the pleasure pocket in the chapter titled "Free Money."

Can a file save you money? Does it pay to be organized? A few months ago I received my monthly bill from the gas and electric company.

That's odd, I thought, it's much less than I usually pay.

I opened my accordion file to "Utilities" and removed the customer's copy of my previous bills.

Something is wrong here. Not only is the dollar amount much less, but the numbers from the meter reading don't make sense. Didn't I use more gas than that last month? I'll go check the numbers on the meter.

I phoned the utility company.

"I want an explanation of my bill." "Oh, the person reading the meter made a mistake, but it will be corrected next month."

"No, I can't accept that. If I am billed at one time for two months use, that total puts me in a higher rate bracket. I want my statement adjusted to show two separate months."

My utility company has different rates depending on seasonal use. There is also a base rate and a higher use rate. If I pay for two months at one billing, I am paying at a much higher rate.

Two minutes to look in my file, plus one phone call, equals dollars not spent. No computer will do that! I made a note to myself, on my check stub: confirm accuracy of next month's bill.

Safe deposit box

Congratulations! You have come a long way in this system already. But you need one more important item at your bank — a safe deposit box. Here's another list. This one is to suggest some of the papers you might own that should go in your deposit box and not in your file.

Certificates of birth, marriage, death and divorce. Copy of your will (note the location of the original on the copy). Insurance papers. Military papers. Securities. Titles to real property (auto, house, etc.). Legal documents. Pension plan.

Make a list of everything you put in your safe deposit box and, for goodness sake, keep it up to date. Where will you put the list? Right. In your file under *PERSONAL*.

If you are not the only person with the right to use this box, make sure your co-owner(s) have actually come to the bank at least once, signed the box entry permit form, used the box, and returned it to the vault. This is a worthwhile exercise since it shows on bank records that all persons entitled to use the box have done so. Their signatures have been accepted by the bank at some time and should there be an emergency, a death, no co-owner will be denied access to the safe deposit box because of an unfamiliar signature.

Some banks charge you a monthly fee for a box. Others give (not really, remember a *piggy bank?*) you a box "free" if you maintain a specified amount of money in the bank. If you actually pay for your box, file the bill under *DEDUCT-IBLES* in your accordion file.

In addition to all the banking services I have discussed, in the previous chapter and in this one, there are bank money market accounts, savings accounts, investment accounts, and many others with names I don't understand. I'm not going to say anything about these because anything I say today is apt to be obsolete tomorrow. Banks are full of change! So much change that often the bank managers themselves aren't sure what services they will be selling a month from now. All I can say is read, compare, learn, and decide what's best for you. And always be willing to change your decision.

Cash "phutt"

I foresee a time, and rather soon, when all banking will be an electronic process. Your checkbook may become a collectors' item of quaint Americana. You will have home video banking and all your personal financial transactions will go phutt, phutt, phutt, in and out of computers. I cringe at the thought! A plastic debit card will be issued at the same time you get a plastic credit card. We will have "cash phutt" instead of "cash flow." However, that is the future. For today you must keep up with the changes as they occur. Not all your decisions and choices, no matter how well thought out they are now, will be valid in your future.

Play it safe

Since you should keep only enough money in your checking account to pay your monthly bills, you do need one other account where you can put at least three months of normal income — a safety account. I think of mine as my survival fund. Should you have an emergency and not have any income for three months, you can still survive.

This safety account does not have to be a passbook savings account. It doesn't even have to be an account in a bank. A credit union or a money market fund usually pays an interest rate higher than a bank provides. Such a fund, or an account, must be in readily available cash and it should be paying you interest. How much? As much interest as you can get as long as it qualifies for the safety and accessability requirements.

Can you believe it finally is time to leave the bank? It is. You have worked hard, learned a lot, and finished the most complicated part of the system. From here on it's a breeze.

No more pieces of paper to drive you crazy. No more worry about your valuable documents and records. Put shoes in your shoe box. Your small file has the canceled checks and bank statements. The large file has all the receipts and record keeping materials. Your checkbook is up to date and the stubs and deposit receipts tell you where your money came from and where it went. . . . Take a break! Go for a walk. Work around the house or yard. Take a nap.

Your notebook

And see if you can find a three ring loose-leaf notebook around the house. One that isn't being used. If not, you'll have to buy one. Buy the cheapest one you can find and also pick up a pack of wide lined filler paper and a package of those stiff, colored paper pages that are called dividers. You'll need a pencil, a pen, and a ruler. When you have those supplies together, and you feel rested, I'll show you how to design your notebook.

4.

Make a Scene

I'm sure you put the cash register receipt from the office supply store into your accordion file pocket under *DE-DUCTIBLES*. It's best to jot a word or two on receipts like that one to jog your memory at tax preparation time.

This next part of the system is enjoyable. I take pleasure in making the pages for my notebook and filling in the information. It's like, well, it's like doing a jigsaw puzzle. Finding all the little pieces, seeing where they fit, putting them in place and sitting back to look at a picture I never have seen before. My scene! The picture of my financial life. My dollar autobiography.

You now have a notebook, filler paper, pencil, ruler, and the dividers in front of you. Imagine — one three ring notebook will replace the confusion of what has been your financial three ring circus!

First, the dividers. On each index tab, write one of the following categories:

1. Support Team.
2. Auto/Transportation.
3. Insurance.
4. Household.
5. Income, Deductibles.
6. Investments.

Next, put about ten pages of filler paper in each section, except for *Household.* You will want about twenty-five in that section.

After you have done that, I'll take you section by section through the notebook, show you how to make the pages for "cash flow," and tell you what information to include in each section. Since you are just starting your notebook, you won't have too much information to include right now. After a few months, even three, you will begin to see the puzzle take shape. This peek at your financial picture is a tease. You'll find you can't wait to enter your figures for the next month, and the next, so you can see more of the picture. If you do not like what you see, don't worry. I will show you some ways to change your picture in other chapters.

Support team

Let's get started on the first section: *Support Team.* Contrary to most of the pages in the notebook, records for each current year, the pages in this section are permanent. They will stay in the notebook for years and years (unless you are a transient). You will notice not only your support team information goes in here, but also all the facts related to the services those team members provide. While the pages are permanent for as long a time as you retain the same members of your support team, the information on the services provided by these experts will, of necessity, show some changes. New information will be added. Obsolete facts will be crossed out. It is impossible to trust your memory with all the vital details and statistics listed on these pages. Nor can you rely upon anyone else to keep these records for you.

The first page, **Lawyer,** is the example for making all the pages in this section.

LAWYER
Name of Firm

Name   Original will on file — 1976
Address   Copy in safe deposit box
Telephone number

That is page 1. Should you have any additional documents or records on file with your lawyer, you would list them on this page.

Page 2. **CPA or tax advisor.** Name, firm name, address, telephone number. List of records on file.

Page 3. **Doctors.** Names, addresses, telephone numbers. List all medical information for all family members such as allergies, inoculations, operations, and their appropriate dates. Dentists and dental records can be included on this page.

Page 4. **Minister, Priest, or Rabbi.** Name, address, telephone number. Burial instructions on file.

In our society today, death is an institutional experience. By that I mean it occurs typically in a hospital or nursing home, only rarely in our own residence. I try to take care of my death with the same concern I give to my life. For that reason I plan on my death. I make sure my religious advisor and my primary physician have instructions, from me, as to my preferences for my dying. I expect these two members of my support team to observe my preferences in the services they provide. I see to it that they are aware of each other now, so they can function in co-operation on my behalf in the future.

Page 5. **Broker, investment advisors.** Name, firm name, address, telephone number. Account number. List of investments held by broker (those not in your safe deposit box). You might consider this list an unnecessary duplication of the investment records you receive from your brokerage firm. Those records are produced by computers! You cannot abdicate your responsibility for your money and assume a machine knows more than you do. Chapter Seven will explain the detailed and explicit records you must keep for every one of your investments. On this page you are simply identifying the investments that are not represented by actual certificates in your safe deposit box.

Page 6. **Bank.** Name, address, telephone number. List of all accounts, account numbers, names on those accounts. Safe deposit box number, names of co-owners, location of box keys. List of box contents (be sure to keep this list up to date!)

Page 7. **Charge cards.** Names of companies and credit card numbers. How to notify issuer if a card is lost or stolen (toll free numbers).

Recently, I have been receiving ads from various companies telling me they will, *for a fee,* be glad to notify all my card issuers for me should I lose a card or have one stolen. What? I am supposed to pay for that? Why can't I look at page 7 in my notebook and dial a toll free number myself? I always get that toll free number when I am sent a new credit card. So far I have not been able to figure out why I should pay someone to make a free call for me. I'm working on it. Nor am I eager to have a list of my credit cards and their numbers neatly listed, along with my name and address, etc., in some company's office files or computer.

Automobile — Transportation

That's the end of the first notebook section. The second section is *Auto/Transportation.* This will include all the information about your car or other transportation you own — boat, bike, airplane. If I owned a model railroad, I guess I would keep those facts and figures here, as well.

Before I list and describe the information you will be recording on the pages in this section, let me ask a question or two. Why do it? Why bother making these pages and writing in such things as serial numbers, telephone numbers, or the identification number of a car key? A few additional questions will be far more convincing, I think, than some simple answers.

Have you ever lost the keys to your car? Have you ever had to fill in an accident report or submit a claim to an insurance company? Have you sold a car or moved to a new state and applied for a license plate? All of these situations involve stress, confusion, and a certain time urgency. Your notebook pages, completed at your leisure and during a period when you are free from anxiety, will be one of the wisest and most rewarding investments you will ever make.

I'll use a car as my example for these pages.

Page 1. Make, model, year. Serial number. Key number (ignition, trunk). Location of duplicate keys. License number.

Page 2. Insurance (all other insurance is kept in a separate section; *all* information on transportation is kept here). Name of insurance company, address, telephone number, policy number. If you have an agent, keep all that information here also. Premium: amount, date(s) due, whether it's annual, semi-annual, quarterly. Location of insurance policy (deposit box). Information on warranties, guarantees for car, tires, battery, etc. Finance information, if any, such as to whom, when, how much, etc.

Page 3. The first two pages in this section will be permanent, more or less. They change only if you buy or sell a car or change your insurance. The third page changes each year. It contains all the records for any one given year. On January first of every year, I go out to my car, read the odometer, and enter that number at the top of this page. Why? A comparison of my annual readings tells me how many miles I have driven in one year. There are some tax implications for that. Deductions for gasoline taxes can be based on "number of miles driven." I can also compare the number of miles I drove a car last year with the miles driven this year. Driving is a luxury — it is expensive.

All miscellaneous automobile expenses are recorded on this third page. For example: AAA dues, parking fees, tickets for violations, date and amount for license and registration renewals. You may need more than one page at this point because here is the place to keep a record of all the service dates and costs for the car. In addition to the dates and expenses for any necessary servicing of your car, include the odometer reading and what service jobs were performed at that time. The expenses for oil and gas go in here.

Here's an example of how these pages might look.

Page 1.

Car #1

1979 Oldsmobile	License number: XYZ123
Model K 87	
Two door Cutlass Supreme	
Serial Number 4K57D8V942784	
Keys: ignition — 76 WB	Duplicate keys in top,
trunk — 94 LR	right hand drawer of desk.

Page 2.

Insurance

Policy in safe deposit box

Premium: $380.00

USBS Insurance Company
444 Center Street
Chicago, IL 87355

Deductible: $500.00

Policy No.: ZX15P37

Phone: (417) 698-4562

Due: November
Pay annually

Agent:
Mr. J. P. Smith
626 Main Street
Hometown, USA 24389

Phone: (419) 896-5468

Battery: One-year warranty; purchased December 1978
Warranty in accordion file
January 1980 — warranty discarded

Page 3.

January first, 1984 — Odometer: 28,670 miles (3249 miles driven in 1983)

AAA dues: Pay in April, 1984 $25.00

Registration: 3/16/84 (deduct) $37.00

Next service due May, 1984, check on right, rear tire

May 5, 1984: Lube, oil, filter change, adjust idle $45.00
30,470 miles

August 9, 1984: Complete service (see records in $128.00
file) 32,720 miles

Next service due November, 1984

Gas-oil

Date   Amount

This section tells everything you ever wanted to know about your car. Well, perhaps not what you wanted to know;

certainly what you should know. It tells you how many miles you drove on a set of new tires. It tells when your car is due for lubrication. Maybe it will tell you to take the car out less often; you're spending too much money on it.

Insurance

Insurance is the third section of your notebook — all the insurance you have except your automobile insurance which you just entered into the previous section. Make one page for each of your insurance policies. All the pages are the same. They look like this: Name of policy, the type of coverage —life, homeowners, renters, condo, health, personal property, etc. The number of the policy, the value of the policy (coverage). Name, address, telephone number of the insurance company. Name, address, telephone number of your insurance agent. Information on the premiums: date due, amount. I include the date and the check number for every insurance payment I make.

The pages in this *Insurance* section are permanent; they are not removed at the end of each year to become a part of your annual file. Insurance is a valuable and essential part of every personal finance plan. It is also responsible for absorbing many income dollars. We need this inclusive and continual picture of our various protection policies so we can evaluate this history of our insurance expenses and estimate future ones with greater accuracy. Unfortunately the future scene usually is one that rises higher and higher and . . .

There are only three more sections in your notebook. *Household* is next and a big part of the puzzle. By now you have had to go outside to look at your car; you have had to hunt for insurance policies; and you have had to write down a lot of facts and numbers. I know that. The first time I set up my notebook I spent many days finding all the information. I will never in my lifetime need to duplicate all that work again.

Along that same line, you may have been muttering and fuming to yourself.

"Sure, write in these numbers. Easy for you to say, Where are all *my* numbers I'm supposed to put in these pages I'm making?"

In your checkbook, on the check stubs.

Finding the facts

Every time you transfer information from your check stubs to your notebook, place a check mark (✔) on the lower, left hand corner of the stub. (See check examples, Chapter Two.) This is an *important* part of the organization system! With one quick look at your stubs, you will be able to confirm that all the facts and figures from your stubs have been recorded in your notebook.

Additional information for your notebook is in your accordion file on the pieces of paper, the receipts, and customer's copies of bills you paid. It does take some time at first to get this system set up, but you have spent much more time, perhaps years, being disorganized. Be patient with yourself. And with me. I promise you, once you put this notebook together, maintaining it will take only a part of the twenty minutes a week recording time I talked about in the beginning of this book.

Do you see what is happening? The pieces of the puzzle begin to make a picture. The scattered financial information is collected. Logic and order replace chaos. It's so easy —once you know how. There are lots of "expert" phrases you could use to describe this system, the process of doing it. You can say, this is an integrated system; interface the file, checkbook, notebook; execute a compilation of materials; meld the components; merge the co-ordinates; a systems analysis. It's fun to play word games with the experts! To repeat *my* words in Chapter One: "You have a system for keeping records."

Household

In spite of the time involved, and the effort, press on. Move right along into the *Household*, Section 4.

All the pages in this section are made the same way. Take your ruler and pencil and divide each page into three long columns, the full length of the page of lined paper. Leave about two inches from the edge of the left hand side of the paper, and run your line along the ruler, from top to bottom. The center column will be around five inches wide. Draw another line. That leaves you with a third column, almost two inches wide, on the right hand side of the paper. On each page, at the top of the first column, write *DATE*; at the top of the second column (the wide one) write *ITEM*; and the top of the third column should read *COST*. Each page will have a different heading. Here are my suggestions for the 18 categories or headings in this section. I also will include some ideas for the kinds of information you will enter under these various headings.

The first page is *MAINTENANCE*. It is the visual aid for all the pages in the Household section.

	MAINTENANCE	
Date	*Item*	*Cost*
1/6/85	repair T.V.	$46.85
3/9/85	trash collection	$ 9.75
3/27/85	back door hinge	$ 4.59
7/2/85	service air-conditioner	$37.36

Obviously there are many other expenses you would include under *Maintanence,* but this visual aid gives you the general idea for the first page.

Here are the headings (categories) for the ITEM columns on the rest of the Household pages. I include some suggestions for the expenses you might enter in these columns.

page 1. *Maintenance*

page 2. *Outside:* yard, fence, dog house, clothes line, plants, flood light, swing.

page 3. *Medical/Dental:* drugs, prescriptions, health equipment, bills

page 4. *Telephone:* bills, purchase, repairs

page 5. *Water:* bills

page 6. *Gas, Oil, and Electric:* bills, deposit receipts

page 7. *Reading Materials:* books, papers, magazines. For all subscriptions, note the period covered by your payments; 1 year, 6 months, etc.

I do not recommend you do this because I want to make extra work for you or because I am a fanatic about records. No, I advise it because it is one more way to conserve money;

to not give away your dollars until it is absolutely necessary.

Have you ever noticed that you receive a subscription renewal notice several months before the actual expiration date? Most people open the notice, see the words, "send money at once or your subscription service could be interrupted," and immediately mail a check to the company. How does this affect your finances? If you have three subscriptions, each one costing you ten dollars, and you remove a total of thirty dollars from your interest paying account for one quarter of the year (three months), you are denying yourself a legitimate return from your invested capital. Instead of giving away your money before it is necessary, look at this page (7.) in your notebook and write the actual expiration date on the renewal notice. On that date, but not before, write your check and mail it to the publisher. It will take at least a month to clear your account and that, too, will be in your best interest.

> page 8. *Legal Fees:* Tax advice costs can be included on this page.

> page 9. *Tax Payments:* Federal, State, Local, Property. Always make a note of the number of the check used to pay any tax. Should there be any inquiry regarding your payment, you can use this notebook record to identify which check was used for the tax payment in question. It takes only a second to include a check number when you record your tax information but this page can save you a lengthy and frantic search in the future.

> page 10. *Store charges:* credit purchases.

> page 11. *Bank credit card and other general charge card purchases:* American Express, Visa, Diners, etc.

> page 12. *Pleasures:* gifts, Christmas, trips, records, movies, sports, pets, cosmetics, wine and liquor, cigarettes, beauty parlours, health clubs, social clubs, parties — oh, what an endless list of all the things we want, but do not need. Be honest on this page.

page 13. *Rent or mortgage payments. Homeowners dues. Association fees.*

page 14. *Food:*

page 15. *Education:*

page 16. *Dues:* clubs, union, professional.

page 17. *Loan agreements* and *installment payments:* all, except auto.

And the last page (18.) is *Home Improvements.* This page is a permanent part of your notebook. Enter all the items you buy for your house that will be a permanent part of the structure, or will remain with the house when you sell it. For example, a patio or porch, a light fixture, built in bookcase, bathroom fixtures. Any expenses that contribute to the capital investment in a property will affect your ultimate tax liability when the day comes for you to sell your last home. This is a book about money (I've said that before), and not about taxes. It's impossible to talk about money and not refer to taxes, but for now my remarks on the importance for this page must be taken on faith. It is an important record! Someday find the time to read about the tax laws for selling a final shelter. Ask your tax adviser.

Four sections down and two to go. *Please* stay with it. Don't be discouraged if there are some pieces of information you can't find right now. Don't let that stop you from collecting the rest of the information and setting up your system.

General income
Section 5 is short and simple. It has, really, two parts to it. On the first page list all your income — *all except dividends and interest.* Investment income is recorded in the last section of your notebook. If you're one of the lucky ones, you might need many pages for income. I need one.

Deductibles
The second page, *Deductibles,* is a "catch-all" for the "D's" on your check stubs that don't fit into any other category. Here you might include: child support; alimony payments; contributions to charities, religious groups, non-

profit organizations, educational institutions; losses not covered by insurance; energy saving equipment; business expenses. I include in this section the number of miles I drive for a charity or my own medical and dental care. All transportation (taxis and busses) used to obtain health care, would be included here.

You have done it. Most of the pieces of your financial life puzzle are collected and placed in the notebook. Only the section on *Investment* is left. I saved that one for last since it adds the rosy glow to any financial scene.

Investment income

In this final section, the first page is divided into three columns, just as in the Household section. The three headings for the columns are: *Date, Source, Amount.* This page should capture your total interest as well as your dividends. You might have interest income from a bank account, a "safety fund," a credit union fund or bonds. I hope you have a lot of interest!

Naturally, you will return to your deposit receipts to find the records of this income. They are all there — or they should be.

Income checks should never be *cashed*; they *must be deposited.* Let's say you receive a dividend check from the XYZ Company for $50.00. Suppose, further, that you cash it. The money is spent and you have no record of receiving that income. No written proof! Oh, yes. I know the XYZ Company will send you a report of dividends mailed to you. At the end of every year, all companies send out forms that report dividend income to a stockholder.

Computer error

Does computer error exist? By now you know my answer to that question. If the XYZ Company computer tells me I received $40.00, and my deposit receipt shows I had $50.00, I can "talk back" to that computer. Should it be deaf, I can at least be assured the IRS gets the true message.

I am not prejudiced. Let's assume the computer did a fine job of reporting my dividend income but the post office lost the form sent by the XYZ Company. Now where am I? No record at all. Not unless I have my deposit receipt, stapled to my check stub, showing me I received the $50.00 dividend. My notebook verifies the receipt, the date I received the dividend, and what company sent it to me. I know everything!

By now I'm sure you are convinced you should fill out these pages.

Current investment transactions

The same line of reasoning will convince you to fill out the second page in this Investment section. There are *four* columns for this page. They read: *Date, Transaction* (buy, sell, deposit), *Amount, Capital gain or loss.* The information you record here is essential for tax preparation. Where will you find the figures for this page? They will all be on the pieces of paper you filed in the Investment pocket of your accordion file. Once you have established your notebook and brought your information up to date for the current year, record all your future investment facts before you file the customer's copy. In this way you effortlessly organize your transactions into chronological order.

It is obvious that it has taken an enormous amount of your time and energy to establish your record keeping system. At this point you may doubt my earlier words when I said it takes only fifteen or twenty minutes a week to *maintain* the system. Not only do I require written proof, I supply it. Here is the routine I follow when I do my own record keeping:

Once a week . . .

1. Pay the bills, fill in the check stubs, note information on my "pieces of paper," balance my checkbook *as I write each check.*

2. Enter all information into my notebook, finding most of it on my check stubs and deposit receipts, and some of it on the miscellaneous forms and papers.

3. File all my receipts, statements, forms, etc.

A clean desk. An uncluttered mind. Peace of mind in return for an investment of seventeen hours a year. That's only a little more than one day out of three hundred and sixty five. What happens to all this financial organization at the end of each year? You guessed it! Now that you qualify as an expert in personal money management, you have one obvious answer: FILE IT!

Peace of mind

Before you read on to the next step in the system, I want to go back to the phrase, "peace of mind." It is difficult to put a value on that kind of a return. Perhaps I can help.

A few weeks ago I spent several hours with a couple who live in a retirement home. They are bright and informed, in their seventies, and have never kept records. They have no peace of mind — far from it! They are worried and confused about their money, legal documents, and their retirement benefits. How do they know if the records from Social Security are accurate? They are faced with major decisions as to where their money should go. For tax reasons, they must know where their money comes from, and when they receive it.

Is it possible to construct a financial life puzzle when most of the pieces are missing? Oh, it is not.

I wish they were the exceptions. My experience tells me otherwise. You, the reader, may be in your twenties, thirties, or fifties. You may not believe you will be seventy-five. You will (if you are lucky).

Keep your records. Establish and maintain this system. This is one of the greatest gifts you can give yourself — certainty about your money. Before you begin the new year, it is time to organize the current one in such a way that it *guarantees* you peace of mind.

5. Happy New Year

You don't need paper hats, noise makers, or champagne for this New Year's celebration. I have in mind a quiet, more subtle occasion. A silent tooting of your own horn in self-recognition of all you have accomplished. Whether you realize it or not, this New Year finds you well on the way to being your own expert money manager.

Your financial diary

Ultimately, money management is far more than a system for the collecting and organizing of facts and figures. Your money is an honest reflection of your life. A picture as accurate as one taken with a telephoto lens. Your body, emotions, and intellect are portrayed in your financial records.

Another way to look at your records, is to see them as a financial diary. In this diary there is no place for fantasy and fiction. The "I wish" and "I hope" are never in the records. Only realities are recorded. The values and priorities of your living mirror the dollars and cents filed in your accordion file, written in your notebook, and entered on your check stubs.

Similarly, in the spirit of the New Year, think of your resolutions for the year ahead. Changes in your financial diary are possible. You can control your money and by using that control you can change some of the wishes and hopes into financial reality.

New Year's resolutions

As I take you, step by step, through the process of making your annual file, look at all your records from the year just finished. Do they reflect your goals? How can you reach your life goals by making change — changes in the way you use your money?

New Year's Eve is a fine time to write down your goals. Ask yourself, "What do I really want? Where do I want to be, financially, in five years, ten, twenty years? How can I get there?" Let your past records be the compass for your future. I suspect you notice a sense of confidence, energy, and self-esteem, that comes from the realization of being in control of your money. You have put an end to the chaos!

Furthermore, as you look at your goals and set up a plan for reaching them, ask yourself, "Are there aspects of my financial life that I want to re-direct? That I can re-direct?"

Planning is not just an exercise on paper; it saves you money. It also prevents headaches, hysteria, fear, panic, and sometimes, domestic discord. The preventatives I have just listed, are obvious. How can planning actually save money? Let me give you an example.

A profit plan

If you own a home, you receive a bill for property taxes. The total amount, if it is paid annually (one lump sum), is usually less than the total amount paid on a semi-annual basis. You know this tax bill is coming. Plan for its arrival. Set aside the tax money you owe, and you end up paying the total once, and for less.

The "pay once and for less" plan will always save you money. Plan in advance, pay in total, bills from stores (no finance charges), insurance premiums, and all credit card statements. I have never understood why people who have an interest in dollars, give their dollars away as interest.

Planning not only saves you money, it earns you some. Dollars you set aside each month, as a plan for paying an anticipated annual expense, can be accumulated in an account paying you interest. Now *that* I understand.

With these ideas in mind, it is time to put away the year just passed and to get on with the new one. From now on, your annual files are the chronological records of your paper past.

Your annual file

This annual file, the first of many that you will make over the years, is again one of your deductible purchases from the office supply store. It, the file, should be the size of your accordion file but this one will have only one open space, or pocket. It should cost about $2.15. Your small file for canceled checks and bank statements had only one open pocket, and by now you are familiar with that one.

Canceled check file

The first items you put into your annual file are the total contents of your small check file. If you always have kept those statements and canceled checks in chronological order, all you need to do is put a rubber band around them and drop them into your file. The small check file is now empty and ready for the New Year.

Step number two. Open your checkbook, remove all the used check stubs and deposit receipts, put a rubber band around them, and drop them into your annual file. Your checkbook is ready for the New Year.

I might mention here, I never buy rubber bands. I remove them from newspapers, find them on the floors of banks, or pick them up off the sidewalk. Many free things are available; I seize all of them!

Accordion file contents

I sit on the floor for the third step. I find that's a comfortable and easy way to spread my records out around me and sort them into chronological order as I review the information. Open your accordion file and remove the contents of the first pocket. Go through these *Auto/Transportation* records. Some of them — the permanent or on-going records — will be returned to your accordion file as a part of your paper present. These would be the copy of your auto insurance, any guarantees or warranties still in effect, or papers you have involving current purchase agreements for your car or other vehicles you own. The rest of your records, the ones relating to only the past year, are fastened together with the free rubber band, or free paper clip . . . Should you wish to be extravagant, you can put these records in a small plastic bag before you place them in your annual file.

Continue to go through each category of your accordion file. Review and update the contents, return any records that apply to the year ahead, secure the current records into one contained packet and drop them into the annual file. Your annual file is bulging. And your accordion file is getting thinner and thinner.

If we were in a class together, this is the time when several hands would be raised. I'll answer those questions now. They all begin with the words: What do I do with the contents of the file pocket labeled _____ ?

INVESTMENTS: Remove all records of investments. Do *not* put them in the annual file. Set them aside, in a very safe place, and in Chapter Seven I will tell you how to set up a special record keeping system for investments.

WARRANTIES/GUARANTEES: Remove all of these. Do *not* put them in your annual file. Find a sturdy plastic bag, preferably one with a handle, and place all the warranties and guarantees for things you bought this year, in the plastic bag. I have a hook on the inside of the door to a downstairs storage closet. I hang my plastic bag on that hook. You could keep this bag in a kitchen drawer or cupboard. Up-date the contents every New Year. Discard any warranties or guarantees that are no longer in effect. I keep maintenance and repair instructions in this same plastic bag. For example, say you bought a new electric blanket this past year. A brochure came with that blanket including laundry instructions, safety information, and repair facts. This brochure, along with the manufacturer's warranty, is placed in the plastic bag. I write, on the outside of the brochure, the date of my purchase and where I bought the blanket.

INVENTORY/PHOTOS: The contents of this section do *not* go into your annual file. I keep a separate, large manila envelope for these records. I have made a list of everything I own. I also have photographs of the contents of my shelter. Making this written and photographic inventory is a good rainy Sunday activity. Actually, I spent several rainy Sundays making my inventory. Begin in the bathroom; it's easy since there isn't much there to record. Maybe an electric razor, hair dryer, hamper, a scale. You'll have to guess at the original price for these items if you don't have back records as a reference. Now continue, room by room, in the same manner, listing the contents and your estimates for the date and price of these purchases. Once the list is finished, do a photo inventory.

Stand in the middle of each room, and using a flash attachment, snap pictures of each area. In the kitchen, just open cupboards and snap away. Do the same for closets and drawers. When the film is developed (deduct this cost) order two prints of each picture. Make a duplicate of your written inventory. My list and one set of pictures is in my house, in my manila envelope. I gave the duplicates to a "buddy." I will introduce this person in the last chapter. Each new year I up-date my household inventory by adding the information from the inventory section of my accordion file. Be sure to cross out the things you have sold or given away during the past year. From this time on it will never be a case of guess work.

You know when you bought something, how much you paid for it, and where you bought it. This is invaluable written proof for an insurance claim, or for the eventual sale of these items. I do not give my inventory to my insurance agent, nor do I put it in my safe deposit box. Again, another part of my private life I want to keep private. Only my "buddy" knows.

SAFE DEPOSIT BOX: Review the list in your accordion file. Make a New Year's visit to your box. Check the box contents and make sure your list is up to date *before you return it* to your accordion file. While you're going over the papers in your box, take time to read the copy of your will. Does this vital document need to be changed in any way? Should you add a codicil?

That concludes the question and answer period. With the exceptions of the three categories, *Investments, Warranties/ Guarantees, Inventory/Photos,* the rest of the papers in your accordion file either are placed in your annual file, or returned to the accordion file. Compare all your current file records with the information in your notebook. This is an "end of the year" safety check to make sure you did not overlook the entry of any information.

General credit card statements

Pay particular attention to the statements from your credit card records (file section #18). A variety of goods and services appear on these statements and you may have overlooked a deductible item or forgotten to record individual expenses in your notebook. Now your accordion file is ready for the new year too.

Finally we get to the notebook. You have just compared the information from your accordion file with the records in your notebook. You can be confident that no information has been lost to you. Not one dollar has escaped your attention. Your notebook pages will be your "work sheets" when it is time to prepare income tax returns.

In spite of the fact that all your dollars are in front of you, they are scattered, fragmented pieces of information. It is time to collect these dollars, put them together, and create a total picture of your money.

The total scene

And total is exactly what you do now. It doesn't matter if you began the system only a few months ago. You may have records for only three or four months — it depends on when you bought this book and began your record keeping system. For now, work with the information you have. Next year you will have the records for a full twelve months.

The first notebook section to prepare for the annual file is the one labeled *Auto/Transportation.* In addition to figures for boats, bikes or planes, the information on your car includes several categories: service, gas and oil, miscellaneous costs (license, registration, etc.), insurance. When the dollars for each category pertaining to your car are added, total all the categories for car expenses. There you have it! The amount it costs you to own a car. Does this number surprise you? A car definitely is a luxury.

As you add the figures within each category and enter the total at the bottom of each column, remove those old pages from your notebook and insert new ones, preparing for the coming year. Out with the old — in with the new! This is an easy way to maintain your notebook.

What's your choice?

I don't want to confuse you over the *Auto/Transportation* section — it's the only complex part of the notebook as it is. However, I feel I must tell you another one of my personal experiences with this system. One that has caused me to make an exception based on my needs.

When I first began this system myself, I removed all the *AUTO* pages and put them into my annual file, along with the rest of my notebook records for each year. I discovered, after a year or two, that I wanted these particular records to stay in my notebook. I wanted to be able to look back one year, two years, more, and compare my costs for all the expenses relating to the ownership of my car. I wanted to have my service records in front of me for the entire period I owned my car. I now keep my records for this section right in my notebook, year after year. I no longer put them in my annual file.

This is another one of those choices I've made based on my own experience and to suit my own needs. This is also another decision for you to make, based on how you want your system to serve your needs.

A fresh start

Prepare the rest of your notebook for your annual file. Continue through all your sections, totaling the numbers in each category, removing the old pages, and replacing them with fresh ones for the new year. Should there by any information you want to carry over into the new year, simply add that to your new page. Obviously there are some permanent record pages that remain in your notebook. You can refer back to Chapter Three if you have forgotten how to "make that scene."

Ultimately you have a series of pages, removed from your notebook, piled on the table in front of you. You are looking at your financial diary. Reality is staring you in the face. No, don't look away. That's not fair. Don't lose hope either. The chapter on "Free Money" will show you how to make changes in your diary if you don't like the way it looks now. You can make those New Year's resolutions come true. Before you clip (free!) your pages together and add them to your annual file, I'd like to suggest some ways you can use this information you have just totaled.

Chart your present . . . and future

January is usually a month of dreary weather, no matter where you live. During the dreariest, most boring weekends, you can find the time to — get ready for this — make some charts. Don't all experts have charts? I like my charts. They show me exactly where my money went, where it has to go, and they help me "chart" my future. I'll show you examples of the charts I make. I keep these in the back of the first section in my notebook, *Support Team.* They are a handy reference for all the decisions I face, and will make, in future years. They are a support, too. They support my informed judgment!

However, I don't want to leave you with your charts, until I have "wrapped up" the annual file. And that is exactly what you do, too. These files usually have a string or cord fastened to them to keep the file closed. If your file is so fat, so bulging with the facts and figures of your past year that the cord won't wrap it up, then find a piece of string and tie the file shut with that. My life, for one year, fits into one file, and is easily tied shut with the attached cord. Perhaps my life is not as exciting as yours. Secure your file the best way you can and in bold, eye-catching numbers, write the calendar year on the front of it. Place this file on a shelf, on the floor of a closet, or any place where it is out of the way — but handy, if you need to refer to it.

Long term storage

How long do you keep annual files? That's a tough question and I hesitate to give an absolute answer. It depends . . . how often do you move, how much storage space do you have, how complex are your finances? One safe answer I can provide — when several files are ten years old, sort through them, remove all records affecting your *future* finances in any way, and place the cumulative, condensed file contents into one inclusive storage file.

I hate to bring up an ugly subject, however . . . if the I.R.S. ever sends you an invitation to an audit, your annual file is your best companion. I've had these taxing invitations and my file of printed proof has always let me attend, and more importantly, leave the situation without any confusion or distress.

On the pages that follow are some of the charts I make. I'll begin with income — I always like that better than expenses.

Income chart

On the Income Chart (pages 64-65), include only the money you receive on a fairly regular basis. You want to know, as accurately as possible, where your income comes from, how much it is, and when you receive it. You are not going to include a once in a lifetime gift of five thousand dollars!

Income is the positive picture of your cash flow — it's all the money entering your financial scene. Chart #2, (pages 66-67) *Expenses,* is the story of your cash flow from a negative point of view — it is all the money rushing away from you. In this instance, the negative is more important than the positive in helping you reach the goal of increased capital because you are in control of the *EXPENSES* Chart. You can make the numbers on the chart become small and smaller, thereby reducing the negative effect they have on your financial future.

Expense chart

To make your *EXPENSES* Chart, use the page headings (categories) and figures from the pages in your notebook. You can see the dollars you are spending each month and you can see which categories cost you the most money during the year.

Your total expenses for the year, from all categories, are in the lower, right hand square.

The moment of truth! Compare total expenses (Chart #2) with total income (Chart #1). I'm saying to myself at this point, "Please let income be greater than expenses." Don't despair if it is not. I have help for you in the next chapter.

Chart #3 (page 68) lets you follow the success of your annual plans for reducing expenses and increasing income. It is possible to set a goal for yourself on this chart but it must be realistic or you will invite discouragement and a sense of failure. You could, for example, decide to reduce your expenses by two per cent next year. If you do not want to work with a per cent of the total, you can concentrate on some dollar figures. Perhaps you could pick ten categories from your expense chart and try to reduce five of them by ten

CHART #1: INCOME

	JAN	FEB	MAR	APR	MAY	JUN
Salary						
Interest						
Dividends						
Etc.						
Total						

JUL	AUG	SEPT	OCT	NOV	DEC	TOTAL

CHART #2: EXPENSES

	JAN	FEB	MAR	APR	MAY	JUN
Automobile/ Transportation						
Insurance						
Maintenance						
Outside						
Medical/ Dental						
Etc.						
Total						

JUL	AUG	SEPT	OCT	NOV	DEC	TOTAL

CHART #3: ANNUAL RECORDS

	1985	1986	1987	1988	1989	1990	1991
Expenses							
Income							

dollars, and the other five by twenty dollars. At the end of the year you will have conserved one hundred and fifty dollars of the money you used to spend. It would take fifteen hundred dollars, invested at ten per cent, to earn you the dollars you removed from your expense chart! The method you use is not important. It is fundamental, however, to decide consciously on a realistic plan, then follow it to success.

Chart #4 (page 70) shows you how much money you will need for *major* expenses — the big ones that occur infrequently (I hope) during the year — and when you will need the money to pay for them. You can anticipate these expenses, and by being ready for them you can "pay once and for less." There will be no need to borrow money or to pay in installments. Our federal government constantly and consistently gives us brilliant examples of the kinds of disasters that can befall the aimless spender.

For a moment, I would like to leave the subject of personal finances and take a look at the condition of government finances. Other than the amount of money involved, I think there is very little difference between the two subjects.

The Grace Commission

In 1983, Mr. J. Peter Grace chaired a panel of highly qualified individuals who were asked to take a very close look at how the federal government manages money — our tax money. This group was officially called the "President's Private Sector Survey on Cost Control." It is more familiarly known as the Grace Commission. What did they do and what did they find out?

They researched the competitive prices for specific necessities (and luxuries) and then compared those prices with the amount the government was paying for the same items. They investigated and identified unnecessary spending. Acutely aware of the devastation created by debt, and the subsequent need to forfeit money in the form of interest payments on the debt, they resolved ways in which present debt could be reduced and future debt could be avoided.

Does this sound familiar? The Grace Commission made a financial diary for the government and the reality is staring in the faces of our elected representatives. Just as the causes and effects in personal money management and government

CHART #4: ANTICIPATED MAJOR EXPENSES

	JAN	FEB	MAR	APR	MAY	JUN	JUL	AUG	SEPT	OCT	NOV	DEC
Taxes												
Insurance												
Tuition												
Etc.												

money management are identical, what Mr. Grace contends is the solution to mismanagement at the federal level is, I believe, no different than the solution for personal finances that are out of control — the solution I refer to as the *paper clip philosophy of finance.*

The Wall Street Journal, in January, 1984, printed a statement by Mr. Grace in which he declared, "I've learned that when you want to cut a budget you have to go not only where the big bucks are, but also nit-pick every expenditure."

I'm not sure that we can persuade the government to reduce the funds spent on paper clips but it might be possible to convince our representatives that we would like them to follow our personal example in the ways they use the money we give them. They might take one less airplane trip, spend a little less on a program here and there, and figure out some ways to reduce our debt.

Library Helpers

In the meantime, we had better get back to our own finances. The charts you make for your personal finances will help you to successfully "nitpick" your way through your own expenses. If you find you like putting your finances into chart form, I suggest you go to the library and look for the business reference section. There are some huge, threatening looking volumes called, "Institute For Business Planning." Find Volume 2, called Estate Planning, and turn to the section titled "Planning Inventory and Presentation." I know the names don't seem to make any sense, don't pay any attention to them — it's what's inside that matters. The ideas are great! There are pages and pages with all sorts of charts for every aspect of personal finance.

While you're in the library, wander over to the section on money, economics, finance. This is a gold mine! There are free books, free magazines, free newspapers — all about money. There is one book in the library that I consider so valuable I will suggest you buy it for a home reference guide. This is *Sylvia Porter's Money Book.* It is available in paperback, and it will be a tax-deductible purchase for you.

I want to get back into the scene with a picture of all you've accomplished so far. It may, at times, have seemed to you that you were piecing together your financial picture puzzle, without understanding how the pieces were joined. You have been the one doing all the work up to now; it's time I did something. Here is a picture of your money management system.

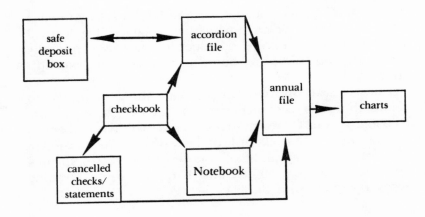

Your New Year's activities have come to a close. You are ready for the year ahead. Just as surely as the paper clip philosophy leads to finance, can income tax returns be far behind? Ah, the joy of the annual file! Considerable time and stress will be avoided when you pull out your file for the preparation of your returns. Your file, particularly those "work sheet" pages, will reduce a torturous task to a painless process. When your returns are completed, file your copies in the annual file for the corresponding year.

In the meantime, the period right after the start of the new year, take some time to study your charts. Compare the figures for income and expenses. How do they match your plans for this year? My plans always include a need, and a want, for more income. I'll assume you're not too different and you would like more money. Is that a safe assumption?

The following chapter suggests some ways you can find more money. I call this "free money," because all you do is find it. It is as free as rubber bands and paper clips; you only have to look for it and it is yours.

6.

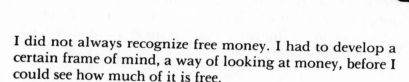

Free Money

I did not always recognize free money. I had to develop a certain frame of mind, a way of looking at money, before I could see how much of it is free.

This frame of mind is the perfect frame for your financial picture puzzle. It is the frame that holds the puzzle in place, that prevents the pieces from breaking apart.

Sand castles

Wanting money is the greatest incentive for finding it. I have never wanted money so I could build little piles here and there, the way children build piles of sand at the beach. They love to scoop up sand and watch it dribble through their fingers as they add a little to first this pile, and then to that one. So intent are they on the little piles, they forget to watch the incoming tide until, whoosh — one unexpected wave washes away all their efforts.

No, I want money for lasting, permanent things rather than piles or castles built of sand. I want a roof over my head, my shelter; I want food on my table, and I want the table to be mine; I want health care when I need it; I want mobility, my transportation; I want to insure my goals, my insurance; and — I want luxuries. I want all the necessities of life for my family and for me, but I also want us to have as many of the luxuries as possible.

The treasure hunt

However, I am a lazy realist — the worst possible combination for a person who wants both necessities and luxuries. I had to find a way to turn "I wish" into "I will;" "I want" into "I have." Will I inherit a lot of money? Not likely. Can I plant a money tree? Will I be appointed president of a corporation? No! And I do not want to work night and day for the rest of my life. I had to find free money. I did. I found it. There is so much of it, I can afford to share some with you. I won't give you the money, but I will tell you where it is. I shall suggest only a very few specific ways to find money in each of the following locations. I do not intend to provide all the suggestions for you. There are hundreds of ways to find free money and they are listed in numerous books on this one subject. My intent is to start you on your money search, to nudge you in the right direction. I want to construct a frame of mind, not a list.

Hidden cash

The easiest way to get more money (experts call this "increasing capital") is to stop giving away so much of what you already have. I call that *limiting the abuse of obtaining necessities*. Fortunately, there are very few necessities: shelter, food, transportation, clothing, insurance, and taxes.

You may wish to argue with me about that list. I can hear your first argument, "You forgot education." No I didn't. Education is a luxury. It is important to discriminate between *I need* and *I want*. We need very little: we want so much.

So, my primary goal is to obtain my necessities with the least number of dollars. It is the luxuries I'm after! I am in competition for the "Worst Consumer of the Year" award. My opponents are all the people in this contest who either try to take my money away from me, or try to persuade me to give it to them. I refuse to give up my money whether through ignorance or negligence.

Shelter

The first place to look for free money is among your necessities. Your shelter contains some of it.

We all have to live someplace — a house, condominium, van, castle, tent, apartment, estate. Moving is so expensive I recommend you stay put and look inside your present shelter for money. Here are some of the ways I find free money in my shelter. They will suggest more ideas to you and soon your imagination will be a printing press cranking out dollars.

Clean money

Cleaning your shelter doesn't have to be expensive, but many people seem to enjoy pouring money down a drain. The shelves in supermarkets and hardware stores have a fortune in cleanliness, lined up in neat row after row. They can keep their fortune; I am building mine. I use vinegar, detergent, ammonia, scouring powder, and once in a while, a little furniture polish. Elbow grease is still free.

Expensive repairs and replacements are avoided by maintenance, by taking care of what you have. Once a year I have a "paint patch" day. I touch up all the nicks and scratches on walls and furniture. I also lubricate everything that moves, so it will keep on moving. I follow the manufacturers' advice on the care of products I own. I "spot clean" carpets, vacuum drapes, turn mattresses — all those good old-fashioned chores that still pay off — in future dollars not spent.

The "bag lady"

Some things I never buy: cotton — it comes in the top of pill bottles; plastic food containers — I save the ones that package the foods I buy. My note pads are scrap paper from everywhere. I never buy paper towels or napkins — drip dry cloth ones are washed "free" in the regular laundry. Everytime I drive or walk near a construction site, I ask the workmen if I may have the small, clean pieces of lumber that are lying around. I use those for repairs, and sometimes for kindling. I always stop and collect pine cones, large branches, logs; fire wood is a great luxury. I rarely buy plastic anything. There is so much money tossed into garbage cans.

I don't want you to think I'm an eccentric "bag lady," so I'm giving you a list of numbers. I try to avoid such lists because none of us remembers them and they usually are boring. I'll risk boredom to prove my point.

30 labels for your accordion file	$ .83
large package of rubber bands	.59
small box of *paper clips*	1.40
package of cotton balls	1.70
1 roll paper towels	.85
1 package paper napkins	1.07
3 plastic food containers (1 quart size)	2.69
	$9.13
tax	.54
	$9.67

The prices are from my local supermarket and chain hardware store. They are the lowest price for each type of goods. Not *one* of these individual purchases is important to the average consumer. But you are above average! You know it takes $96.70 of your invested capital, at 10% interest, to buy these items.

$9.67 is the "tip of the iceberg." Let's turn the numbers around and look at cold, hard cash. $9.67 not spent in one week x 52 weeks a year = $502.84! I'm happy to bend over and pick up a "free paper clip" so I can spend $500.00 on a luxury or buy an investment.

Utilities

Utility companies do not list me among their generous supporters. The dishwasher is turned off *before* the dry cycle — my dishes are dried free. I can read under a cozy, electric blanket for less money than in a cozy, furnace heated house. My oven is never used unless an entire meal is cooked in it, and I usually cook an extra meal free at the same time. One roast chicken in an oven is a lonely sight! I see to it that there is a second one in there to be eaten another day. When I leave town for more than two days, I turn the temperature control on the refrigerator *up*, the one on the furnace *down*, and the one on the water heater, *way down*.

Too much to swallow

Those are just a few of the ways I don't spend money in my shelter. I don't spend money in my stomach, either.

There are so many exciting things to do with money, I

have never understood why so many people eat theirs. They chew up, and swallow, thousands of dollars every year. I enjoy going to the grocery store. My adversaries are there, and I will leave the store victorious!

In Chapter Two, I stated my opinion about carrying (*not* carrying is what I said) a checkbook in your purse or pocket. The most dangerous place to take a blank check is to the supermarket. You have the notion you can buy anything and everything. Take a list, some cash, and be self-limiting in your purchases. This is not a book on nutrition or home economics — I leave that to the experts. However, let me give you a few of my non-spending ideas for food shopping.

I don't buy salad dressing; I make my own from vinegar and oil. I never buy produce out of season. When I had a young family, I bought powdered milk, and cooked cereals rather than dry ones. I buy "day old" bread. If you buy bread on Tuesday, and eat a piece on Wednesday, aren't you eating "day old" bread? Few of us can eat a loaf a day. I never buy frozen, prepared meals. Why not?

The following prices are from a local supermarket.

2 small servings of macaroni and cheese — frozen, prepared	$1.45
6 liberal servings of macaroni and cheese — cook at home (macaroni — $ .77; cheese — $2.73)	$3.50
2 lbs. chicken — frozen, prepared for frying (4 servings)	$3.19
3 lbs. chicken — cook at home (4 servings)	$2.72
2 small "salisbury" steaks, frozen, prepared	$2.99
4 liberal servings, top quality ground chuck, cook at home	$2.15

The important information in this list is:

8 small servings of chicken, ground beef, macaroni and cheese, frozen and prepared come to *$7.63*. (95¢ per serving)

14 liberal servings of chicken, ground beef, macaroni and cheese, prepared at home, come to *$8.37.* (59¢ per serving)

And I hate to cook! But I do it because I would rather take a trip to Hong Kong than eat frozen, prepared "salisbury" steak.

I have a long, long list of food *not* to buy. Supermarkets have aisles I've never seen, shelves I've never touched. How can people work all day to earn money — eight hours! — and then go home and in thirty minutes swallow it?

Or gamble it away! What does gambling have to do with food?

Near the college classroom where I teach, there is a student lounge. A row of food vending machines lines one wall. Most of my classes are held at night; the men and women who attend these classes have already worked a 9 to 5 day. I watch their money, coin after coin, slide into the machines. Playing the "food slots" is a losing gamble. A bet on loss of capital and gain in weight. Mouths *and* machines consume thousands of dollars.

Do you remember, back in Chapter One, when I asked you to think of money as interest? The example I used then, as a way of "seeing" $100.00, was to think of it as $1000.00 invested at 10% interest for one year. Food can earn your interest money for you if you don't have a thousand to invest. Two dollars a week, *not* spent on food, will give you $104.00 a year. $104.00 of free money!

When I do shop for food, I never buy things I can't eat! Health and hygiene needs are purchased at a cut-rate drugstore. Books and magazines are food for thought — they don't belong in a grocery cart.

Co-operative readers

Let me tell you about my non-spending ideas for books and magazines. Three friends and I formed a "subscription pool." We each subscribe to two magazines. That way, the four of us receive eight magazines, which we then share. Eight, for the price of two! My book exchange gives even better odds. The residents of my neighborhood have a "book pool." One neighbor donated some old bookcases. Another donated garage space. We all take our books, the ones we don't want to keep, to the neighborhood free book supply center. Not all the dividends from the "book pool" can be counted in dollars, nor seen in black and white. Conversations take place, mutual interests are discovered, kindness and thoughtfulness are expressed, loneliness and isolation are replaced with companionship and hospitality. The benefits of the "book pool" ripple through all our lives.

Think thin

Somehow, I got rather far from food, but that's the direction I want anyway. Food does take away my money — not only by buying it, but by consuming it. By eating less, I stay thin. Thin is healthier than fat. The excessive number of dollars tucked away in your stomach, usually end up in a doctor's office. You can limit the abuse of another necessity: health care.

And another: clothing. By weighing now, what I weighed at fifteen, I can wear my old clothes. Just as I don't want to eat my money, neither do I want to carry it on my back.

Wardrobe wary

There are many ways to avoid giving away money in exchange for clothes. I bought all my children's clothes at used clothing shops. There are some very elegant ones, especially in large cities. I buy quality T-shirts, jackets, sweaters and sport shirts in stores for young men. Alterations are free! Pockets are real, not fakes. The prices in these stores, often for better quality and workmanship, are far less than in stores for women. Out of style wide ties can become fashionably narrow for a few dollars. The Wall Street Journal carries ads for this reasonable and excellent transformation.

Nor do I pay manufacturers for the privilege of wearing their advertising. If I were going to do that, I would expect them to pay me. Designer labels do serve as status symbols for some people, I suppose, but I would rather increase my status by increasing my wealth.

Your costly key

Indeed, shelter, food, health care, clothing are among the necessities that hold the key to free money. Another key that can help limit the abuse for obtaining yet another necessity, is the one for your car. Everytime you remove the car keys from your purse or pocket, you are removing your dollars. What does it cost you to *own* a car? To drive to the supermarket, hardware store, clothing store? To have insurance, repairs, replacement? The most recent figures I have seen place this cost at about forty cents a mile. What did your odometer reading tell you about the miles you drove this past year? The figures are in your notebook. Multiply that number by $ .40 and you'll see how transportation moves your money out of your billfold.

I know a young woman who has figured out a way to keep her transportation dollars in her pocket. She's the same woman who is now investing her free money. She puts on her jogging shoes and walks to her office. She doesn't spend money on transportation, shoe repairs, or health clubs.

I know we all can't walk to our jobs. And we can't walk to stores and banks and libraries. But we can plan our driving in such a way that we make all these necessary trips at one time. My car spends days and days sitting there — waiting for me to get an errand list finished before it leaves its parking place. When I lived in cities with convenient public transportation, I used trains and busses.

Premium savings

Since I am a realist, I know most of us need a car. And we need insurance. I am constantly comparing the insurance fees of various companies. One way I have reduced the abuse of automobile insurance, is to request the maximum deductibles in my policy. Insurance is one of the necessities that requires serious and informed judgment if we are going to find any free money in this area. Do you always accept the "cost of living" increase on your homeowner's policy? I don't! Most of my household goods decrease in value each year that I own them. I balance my risk of loss, the replacement costs involved, the increase in my premiums, and the current value of my goods before I automatically renew my insurance for a greater amount of coverage.

We have all been told we "need a piece of the rock." Too many of us try to carry an entire mountain. Never automatically renew any insurance policy. Study it. Try to understand the "insiders'" words used in insurance policies. I hate those words! They are confusing and often meaningless to me. But I have attacked my policies with the same zealous intent I use on all my adversaries. I made an appointment with my insurance agent. I asked for explanations of coverage and cost in terms *I* could understand. I read my *Sylvia Porter's Money Book* to see what she says about insurance. I have reduced my insurance costs. Anyone can do it. You must *want* to; it's part of that "frame of mind" I spoke about at the beginning of this chapter.

Never cry "uncle"

Now we come to that final necessity on my list: taxes. My answer to tax abuse is record keeping, vigilance, education, and pragmatism. You have to pay taxes. You must part with your money for this necessity, just as you did for food, shelter, clothing, transportation, and insurance. Use your support team for advice on this one. I believe in experts, and I use them. But I work hard to educate myself and there are many instances when I discover I have learned something the experts don't know.

When I first began my self-education, I read words but didn't know what they meant. I kept on reading. Pretty soon I realized I was understanding some of the words. Then I found out I knew enough to actually question some of the statements I read.

Be patient with yourself. Self-education takes some time, and some effort. It won't be long before you understand all of the "insiders' vocabularies."

In discussing the ways you can find money, I have never used the word BUDGET. I will now. *Don't budget!!* A personal budget is as "realistic" as the federal budget.

The budget myth

If you "budget" $90.00 a month for utilities and the local utility company gets a rate increase, where is your budget? If you "budget" for food and the price of coffee goes way up, or there are floods and storms and the price of food goes way up, where is your budget? If you "budget" for transportation and the cost of gasoline goes up, where is your budget? I could fill pages with examples. A budget, in my opinion, is a time consuming, futile exercise on paper. It never can be realistic because it includes costs over which you have no control. The only valid controls are the ones you set for yourself. A budget tells you what you can spend for things — without telling you what they will cost. Does that make sense? Is it practical to believe your personal budget will control consumer prices? Of course not!

Furthermore, if I have to park my car, I am not going to look in a little notebook to see if the quarter for the meter is "in my budget." I don't want to be bothered with a notebook like that even if it tells me I can park.

A reverse psychology often occurs. Have you heard someone say, "I'm going to buy that. It's in my budget"? We all have seen this attitude in both public and private spending plans. A budget almost commands you to spend money.

There! That is my opinion of a budget. I didn't want you to think I forgot to talk about it. The realistic planning I outline in this book is a flexible system that conserves money. Budget — no. Plan — yes.

What if all your planning leaves you with a "money gap?" What do you do then? Suppose you really need something and you don't have the money to buy it? There are two answers. One involves, what I call, the postponement of "instant gratification." The other involves, (horrors!) debt.

The waiting game

Let's investigate the first answer: instant gratification. This is another frame of mind. It says, "I need it, and I must have it now." Not always. And here I must give you another of my personal examples.

One year, I moved to St. Louis, in the middle of the winter. Frigid temperatures are normal for that time of year. I didn't own a refrigerator, nor did I have any money to buy one. For two months I kept my food on a back porch. During that time I watched for sales of refrigerators and avoided giving away every dollar I could. I finally saw a good sale advertised and I bought the refrigerator — on a regular charge account. That gave me another thirty days to complete my purchase fund. The refrigerator was mine. I had waited only two months before I owned it, but I had three months in which to prepare to pay for it. I did not pay an interest charge, nor a time payment charge. I was not ashamed to be too poor to buy a refrigerator. I have never been victimized by the expectations of society.

Here's another example. This one involves instant gratification, debt and interest payments. I recently noticed an ad for a television set. It stated: T.V. on sale, $329.00. Or, twelve months for $33.00 a month. My arithmetic tells me that if I buy the T.V. over a year's time, I will end up paying $396.00 for it. Should I give $67.00 of my money to some company so I can watch T.V. right now? Or should I wait one year, pay myself the $33.00 a month, put that money in my interest paying account, and at the end of the year I can pay cash for a television on sale and likely have some money left over. Instead of paying interest to someone else, I earned interest for myself. I never was in debt.

Debt

There are times, emergency situations, when you must borrow money. You are in debt. The first thing to do: plan to pay off the loan, plan to get out of debt! You must find your "free money" and use it, first of all, for the debt.

With the exception of a home, or an expensive education, your plan for paying back a debt should be limited to a few years; three years at most. Visit your bank, and talk to your banker. Find out what terms he/she will be able to give you. (There's that word "give" again. Oh well, you know what I mean.) Find out how much interest your bank will charge you for borrowing money. Then shop around. Talk to other bankers. Compare their rates. You are "buying" money: not friendship. Be sure you understand the words, every word, on any loan agreement you sign. Don't be embarrassed to say, "I don't understand." It is your money you're talking about; you should know everything about it.

Credit

The subject of debt involves the word credit. Each of us has a credit rating. All the information about the ways we use money, the information all stores, banks and companies know about our money, is collected and stored in a computer. That machine knows where we live, when we pay our bills, and whether or not we are in debt. It is your legal right to inquire about this private (not really) information. It is your responsibility to know if the financial facts about you are correct. With printed proof, you can change these facts if the computer has made a mistake. Look in the yellow pages of the telephone book, under Credit Bureaus or Credit Reporting Agencies. Phone one of these companies and find out how you can get a copy of your own credit record. I do this about every five years — and yes, I *have* discovered errors.

Your credit rating is established, to a large extent, by the way you use your credit cards. I'm aware many books on money, usually the ones that tell you to budget, recommend you do not have credit cards. Their reasoning for this is, if you have a credit card, you will buy things you do not need or cannot pay for. That line of reasoning would have you believe you never should drive a car because you might exceed the speed limit. Or that you never should take an aspirin because you might take too many.

Credit cards

Again, I don't agree with that advice. I consider credit cards a necessity. By scanning my current monthly charge receipts, I know the exact amount of my outstanding debt at all times. My cards let me leave my money in an interest paying account long after I have made a purchase with them. Credit cards let me carry only a limited amount of cash in my billfold and the receipts provide my sales tax record for each year. They give me financial protection in an emergency. They do all this and more under one important condition —I use them wisely. Any of you, reading this now, is a person who knows how to use credit to your advantage: not to your detriment. I need not say more on this subject!

Once upon a time — fairy tales begin with those words —once upon a time banks issued free credit cards. We leave the make believe story to the story tellers. In the real world we must pay an annual fee for a credit card. You do recall the "piggy banks?" This fee for buying a credit card is, I think, worth the cost.

One of the reasons, in addition to all those I have just mentioned, is that a credit card gives you some of the valuable written proof you want. In addition to my bank card, I have quite a few others. Most of these are issued to me free, but that probably is going to change too! I use my telephone credit card for long distance calls; that has been helpful in several emergency situations. I plan my major purchases (such as the refrigerator) so I can take delivery of the product thirty days before I am billed for it. If I want to order something from an out of town company, I use their free "800" number, state my order, and give them my credit card number. They mail me my purchase and while I had to pay the shipping charges, I did not pay local sales tax. I did not drive my car to a store, I did not pay a parking charge, I didn't even use a 20¢ stamp for a mailed order.

Fairy tales include bad things that happen to people. The bad thing that is going to happen to me is, I suspect, I will have all my credit cards taken away from me. Maybe not all; maybe I still will have one or two. Nobody wants to give me (or you either) thirty or forty free credit days. Electronic exchange of money already is in effect in many areas. The "cash phutt" is almost upon us.

Buy without spending

In the business of money, insiders use another expression: "cash float." Here is my fourth grade way of thinking about the "float." I buy a television set, using my credit card, on the second of May. I don't receive the bill for the set until May thirtieth. I still have several more days before the bill is considered overdue and I will be charged an interest fee on any unpaid balance. All those days — the ones during which I had the set, but had not spent my money to pay for it — are the same days my money is earning interest for me in my account. I have used the "float." To explain this word in one sentence, I might say, "the float is money you use, but don't spend." Anyway, the electronic transfer of money is going to "sink the float." You'll be using your debit card when you make a purchase and your money will instantly leave your checking account. In the meantime, I will continue to use the float in every way I can.

And I will continue to read, to study, to keep informed of all the changes in money.

Finally, I want to make some comments on this chapter. I like organization. I want to see parts and pieces, and how they combine to make a whole. The first five chapters in this book take you on an orderly, logical, section by section process through the organization of your personal finances. They explain a method for keeping records. They involve facts and numbers.

Capital conservation

On the other hand, this chapter involves concepts. True, I use specific examples to suggest ways you can obtain your necessities — shelter, food, transportation, clothing, insurance, taxes — with the fewest number of dollars. In the most brief mention of debt and credit, I do use concrete examples. Or, I should say, for the credit cards, plastic examples. But this chapter, while made up of all these separate parts, is an entity focusing on a basic philosophy of money.

Fundamental and historical doctrines have come under this chapter heading of *Free Money*. They may seem old-fashioned and simplistic when compared to the "swinging" theories of our modern economy. I am absolutely convinced they are as valid today as they always have been.

"Do not live beyond your means. Waste not; want not. Don't buy it if you can't pay for it. Be thrifty, frugal. Don't throw away your money. Save. Necessities before luxuries. Be prudent. Make do with what you have. A dollar saved is a dollar earned."

The list is endless. and in a way, so are the results from practicing this "paper clip philosophy of finance."

Once you have stopped giving away money, it won't be long before you will have collected a surplus — extra dollars that aren't needed for necessities or your safety fund. These surplus dollars — the "free money" you found in your present income — are the ones you can invest. Invested money provides luxuries and a secure retirement.

Robert Z. Aliber, a professor at the University of Chicago School of Business, and an authority on International Economics and Finance, has written a book, *Your Money and Your Life*. I am delighted to find this distinguished scholar and I agree about the value of money *not spent*. Professor Aliber explains how even a few dollars withheld from spending are the equivalent of a return from a sizeable capital investment. Don't let his impressive credentials intimidate you. This is a book everyone can and should read.

Hidden resources

While you are in an investment frame of mind, I want to follow a few of your unspent dollars — some of your "free money" you used to eat, wear, and give away. These are only a very few of the dollars that ease you into a cash situation and then propel you into investing.

Money not spent on:	Amount each month:	Total in one year at no interest:
Food	$ 7.00	$ 84.00
Transportation	$ 2.00	$ 24.00
Clothes	$ 5.00	$ 60.00
Pleasures	$10.00	$120.00
Phone, gas, electric	$ 2.00	$ 24.00
	$26.00	$312.00

If you don't spend the few dollars each month, they add up to $312.00. That's easy to see. What happens in a year if you put those same dollars into an account that pays 8% interest, and the interest is compounded every month?

Food	$ 87.15
Transportation	$ 24.90
Clothes	$ 62.25
Pleasures	$124.50
Phone, gas, electric	$ 24.90
	$323.70

How much money (capital) would you need, paying 8% interest, to earn you $323.70 at the end of one year? $4037.50! What happens to those twenty-six dollars not spent each month, if they are invested at the same 8% interest, compounded monthly, and *five* years go by?

Food	$ 514.36
Transportation	$ 146.96
Clothes	$ 367.40
Pleasures	$ 734.80
Phone, gas, electric	$ 146.96
	$1910.48

One less movie, one less tie, $2.00 less on gas, a letter instead of a phone call . . . in five years the monthly conservation of a few dollars will produce almost two thousand dollars.

Some of you may not think $1910.48 is much money, especially if it took five years to accumulate it. Would you like to have $23,881.00? That is how much capital you need to produce (still at 8% interest) the $19110.48 at the end of five years.

How long will it be before you have dollars to invest? I don't know. It depends on how much you used to give away, or wear, or eat. It depends on your evaluation of "I need" as opposed to "I want." It depends a great deal on how you judge instant gratification.

Despite the fact that I can't tell you *when* you will have surplus money to invest, I *know* you will have it.

Establishing your money management system, maintaining it, setting realistic goals, making flexible plans — these lead straight to investment capital. The need to invest is one of the conditions that results from financial organization. The elimination of financial chaos places you in a cash situation. Soon you will be studying books on finance, not money. It happens. There is no way to avoid it.

To help you in your transition from money to finance, I have included a brief chapter on investments. I do not teach where to invest; there are experts (and some not so expert) who lecture and consult on that subject. I will show you how to keep your investment records.

If you are an experienced investor, you will want to skip the first few pages and turn directly to the information on records and organization.

7.

Your Investments

Mark Twain remarked that an uneducated risk (he called it speculation) in investments takes place under two conditions: when a person can afford it, and when a person can't afford it.

Since all investing involves risk, the key word in the Twain philosophy is *uneducated*. How can that be translated into educated? There are several ways, and fortunately, most of them are free.

Free advice

There are radio and television programs on investing. The daily newspaper has a business section, and papers such as *The Wall Street Journal* and *Barron's* are almost wholly devoted to business, money, and investing. These last two papers, along with shelves and shelves of books, are available to you at the library. Local community colleges have courses in finance.

I have tried *not* to recommend books for you to buy. That is in keeping with my non-spending frame of mind. However, I have suggested you buy one or two, and I now propose a third purchase: *How to Buy Stocks* by Louis Engel. This excellent book, paperback and tax deductible, should be on every investor's book shelf. The title is misleading. It does much more than tell you about buying stocks. It tells, in an easily readable and understandable way, what the stock market is all about. It teaches you the "insiders' vocabulary" for the investment business.

Another way to become educated about investing, is to phone all your local investment companies, the brokerage houses, and ask to be put on their mailing lists. Tell them you are new to investing and want to be notified of any classes or programs they sponsor. You will soon have more information than you can possibly absorb.

Money talk

At first the words you read and hear might seem to be a foreign language. The business of finance is conducted in slang. We all learned, and used, slang expressions when we were children and teenagers, so this is nothing new. You will pick up all these strange words very quickly. They are rather fun to know and use.

A few weeks ago I was in a brokerage house. I saw a word on a computer I didn't understand. I asked a broker,

"What does that mean? I never have seen that word before."

"I'm not sure," he replied, "but I know where I can look it up if I ever need to find out."

This broker has been in the investment business all his life. I admire and respect his knowledge and ability.

The point I'm making is, not *all* the words are important. You do not have to know everything before you invest. This self-education process goes on forever. I have been an investor for many years — and I still have a lot to learn.

Visit a brokerage house. Walk right in and say,

"I don't know much about investing. I want to learn. Do you have any printed information I may have? Will you explain the ticker tape?"

Get acquainted with someone in the office. There are very nice people working there and not all of them are busy all the time. Someday one of these brokers (another name is account executive) will be *your* broker, and you will be helping him or her earn a salary. Your broker is one of your support team, that group of experts you hire and from whom you get advice so you can make your own decisions. Be kind to all these people; allow them to show you how much they know. If you don't understand something, say so.

One more thought on brokerage houses and then we will move on. I think any form of the word "broke" is an unfortunate choice when it is used in connection with money. Especially my money. It makes me nervous.

Why diversify

There is a common investment concept which, I think, has considerable merit — diversification. I invest the same way I buy the tools in my garage. If I am going to repair a warped fence, replace grout and install a new pane of glass, I need a variety of tools. I can't accomplish any one of these jobs with only an assortment of screwdrivers, no matter how fine and extensive is my screwdriver collection. I will need a hammer, nails, putty and, of course, experience.

Mutual funds

Finances are tools — and eventually you will want a variety for the job at hand. How do you buy a variety of financial investments (diversify) if you have a most limited amount of money? One way is to buy a mutual fund. That's like buying a tool kit; an assortment in one package with a single purchase.

As tool kits vary in composition and quality, so do mutual funds. Sometimes you must pay a broker's commission to buy a fund. Those are called "front-end" mutual funds. A "no-load" fund is one you buy without a commission. I don't know where these descriptive (slang) terms originated and I don't care. I do care to know what a mutual fund will cost me and "what's in the tool kit."

How do you find information on these funds? Your broker can tell you about the ones he sells; naturally they are the ones requiring a commission. *Barron's* (in the library) has ads for the no-load funds and usually the free "800" numbers are included in the ads. Phone the companies, ask to have information sent to you, and become familiar with these investment tools.

Stocks

Let's assume you have spent several months learning about investments. It's time to consider spending some of that free money of yours. It's been in an account, or money fund, earning you more money while you became educated. You have met several brokers and have decided which one you want to work for you. Phone the firm, make an appointment, tell your broker how much money you want to spend, listen to her or his advice.

Then go home.

The right track

Don't be in a hurry to spend your money. Think about the advice. Perhaps three different stocks have been suggested to you. Now begin to study and learn about these particular companies. Make a chart! Twice a month, look in the paper and write down the selling price of these stocks. That's called "tracking a stock." Watch for any articles about these companies. Get acquainted with them; find out all you can before you write a check.

Would you invite a total stranger to live with you, to share your home and your life? You don't want to take in an unfamiliar investment and make it a part of your financial life either.

On pages 94-95 is an example of a chart you can use to track your stocks (watch the price changes). There are psychiatrists who believe that, for some people, money is erotic. For most of us, however, money is erratic and there is no better an illustration for this than the ups and downs of the stock market. By charting (tracking) the fluctuations of the stocks you want to own, you can buy a stock at a comparatively low price rather than when it is selling at its all time high one.

Twice a month, write in the price at which the stock closed (the final price at the end of a day). The last column shows the yearly high and low price for each stock. By now you know this information is in the newspaper or a *Standard and Poor's Stock Guide*. (They have done it again — a stock guide with the word "poor" in it. Now we have "broke" and "poor" used in connection with money!) You will get to know the habits of these stocks, and you can compare your informed judgment with that of your account executive.

Keeping your shares

Eventually you are ready to write a check and buy shares in one company. You will receive a stock certificate proving you own those shares. What will you do with it? You have two choices.

You can let your broker keep it for you. That's called leaving your stock in street name. Or you can put it in your safe deposit box. There are advantages, and disadvantages, to either choice. This is not a book on investment advice, so of course I cannot give you all the reasons for making your decision. I do urge you to read about the differences between these two systems. Since I prefer to be in control of my investments, as I am in control of my money, I keep all my stock certificates, bonds, partnerships, etc. in my own safe deposit box.

Whichever choice you make, you will have to keep records. I am not saying you should, or you can, I am saying you *must!*

You must know the date of every investment you buy, how much you paid for it, when it returned income to you, and how much that income was. You must know exactly when you sell an investment, how long you owned it, and how much money you sold it for. You should know how much commission you paid on any financial transaction, and any taxes you paid.

"What — I have to know all that?"

"Oh, yes. And more."

I will give you the basic investment records you need to keep you on the road to riches and retirement.

One question is asked in every one of my classes and by every one of my clients: "How long do I have to keep investment records?" There is no easy answer. It depends on the records. My personal rule: Keep every record that can affect, in any way, my taxes during my lifetime.

Gain or loss

When you made your notebook, you included a section for investments. There was one page, divided into four columns, for transactions in the current year. I did not explain the importance of the final column, the capital loss or gain records, because I felt it would make more sense to you if it were discussed in this chapter.

A loss or gain from your investment transactions influences your income taxes. The figures from a capital loss or gain are not limited to one year; they can be carried over into future years. You will want advice from your tax expert on this subject.

However, that expert cannot help you if you don't know all the dollar figures involved in your investment decisions. *You* must be the record keeper.

STOCK PRICE TRACKER

Company Name	JAN	FEB	MAR	APR	MAY	JUN
1.						
2.						
3.						

JUL	AUG	SEPT	OCT	NOV	DEC	HIGH/LOW

At the top of the notebook page (see Chapter Four), on the right hand side, record your total loss or gain from the previous year. Much the same way you record the odometer reading each new year in the *Auto/Transportation* section of your notebook.

Obviously, each time you sell an investment you either will make money (gain), or lose money (loss). If you began the year with a gain, you add all further gains to it. Subtract all losses. This allows you to be informed of your tax situation, and how you are doing in your investing as the year progresses.

Here's an example.

Investment section of your notebook.
Page two: Transaction records

+ $2000.00 — 1984

Date	Transaction (buy, sell, deposit)	Amount	Capital gain or loss
2/5/85	sell 50 shares, XYZ Company	$1850.00	Gain: $750.00
			(+ $2750.00)
6/9/85	buy 100 shares, TBC Company	$1600.00	
9/1/85	sell 100 shares, LMO Company	$ 800.00	loss: $1500.00
			(+ $1250.00)
9/6/85	deposit in safety fund	$ 400.00	

Now, that's a terrible example in the sense that it has you losing $1500.00 on the sale of a stock. That *can* happen, you know! Look at the top of the gain/loss column. You began the year with a $2000.00 gain, carried over from the previous year. On your first sale in the year, you made $750, and added it to your total at the top of the page (+$2750.00). The next sale was in September, and you lost $1500.00; subtract the loss from the current total (+$2750.00), and you now have a total gain for the year of +$1250.00. This system is maintained much the same way you keep a running balance in your checkbook.

How do you know whether you have made or lost money on a sale? Where are the records for every stock you own? In the investment folders I will describe.

Individual stock records

In addition to the current records in your notebook, you need a way to organize all the information, for each one of your investments, as long as you own them. I have stock records, still in use, that go back twenty-five years — to the time I first bought the stock.

Pages 98-99 show a sample of my stock record page. You will need one of these for each company you own. I keep each record page in a separate folder. These folders are called report covers and cost about $1.00. The cover is plastic. You can read your stock records without opening the folder and that comes in mighty handy when you have many folders. I keep my folders in alphabetical order, by the name of the company. These folders will hold the records you remove from your accordion file pocket labeled *Investments* at the end of every year. They will hold any articles you find and want to save, that are important information about your investment. They can be the place you put quarterly and annual reports until you have time to study them. Add any letters or communications from the officers of the company in which you have invested.

Bond records

Not all of your investments will be in stocks, although that is what most people buy at first. Someday you will want to keep records for the bonds you own. There is an example for those on pages 100-101.

After all you have learned in the previous chapters of this book, you are not going to buy one of those expensive record keeping books, are you? The ones with fancy gold letters on the fake leather covers? I knew you wouldn't; I was just testing. Make your own. Copy my example on a sheet of typing paper or simply run off duplicates of the pages in the book at your local copy store. Cost? About four cents apiece.

STOCK RECORD

Company Name: _____

Stock Purchases

Purchase Date	Number Shares	Cert. No.	Cost per per share	Total taxes & misc.	Total cost	Avg. Cost per share	Sale Date	Total Sale	Net gain/loss

Stock Dividends and Stock Splits

Date	Rate	New Cert. Nos.	Orig. Purchase Date of stock	New Total	No. Shares	New Avg. Cost Per Share

BOND

Company Name _____   Matures _____

Date purchased	Amount	Current value	Interest Dates	Annual Income	Date Sold	Amount

Happy returns

Now suppose you have done all the things you have read about in this chapter. You educated yourself about investments, you have invested some of your money, and your record keeping system for these investments is completed. Have you thought of what you will do with the interest or dividends from your investments? You have, in my opinion, three choices.

Dividend reinvestment

You can spend the income. I hate that choice, at least for now. The day for luxuries is still ahead. Not far, but not yet. You need to increase your capital during the early stages of an investment program.

You can choose to have all your dividends reinvested in more stock of the same company. This is done for you, at your request, by the company. You never see the income; it keeps growing and growing into a larger investment. Or you can receive the income and put it in an interest paying account or fund until you have enough money to buy shares in another company. I like both of these last two choices.

Should you choose to have your dividends automatically reinvested, it's true that you will not receive a check for those dividends but that does not mean you didn't receive the money. Confusing? Not really.

Imagine, if you will, that you bought twenty-five shares of the XYZ Company. Each quarter of the year (every three months) the Company pays you, the stockholder, a dividend. Imagine further that the amount they pay you is $7.80 a quarter or a total of $31.20 for the year. The Company won't mail you a check for $7.80 but every three months they will take your $7.80 and buy more stock for you. Your dividend might buy only a part of one share, say one half a share. The XYZ Company will apply every penny of your dividend money toward your purchase of more shares.

They also will send you a statement each quarter that shows what the price of the stock was when your purchase was made, how many shares you bought, and the total number of shares you now own. Keep every one of these statements! File them in your stock record folder for the XYZ

Company. Write the information on your stock dividends record sheet (shown on pages 104-105) exactly as you would had you actually received the check and bought the stock yourself. Why? Because as far as the I.R.S. is concerned, you did receive a cash dividend and you must report that income and pay tax on it. Furthermore, whenever you sell these shares, just as you must for any stock you sell, you will have to know the purchase price of the shares in order to figure out whether you have a capital gain or loss.

As you read this, you may think the record keeping is such a nuisance that it is foolish to bother with an automatic dividend reinvestment plan. If there were not some worthwhile advantages, I would have to agree with you. What are the advantages?

Reinvestment advantages

One advantage is — you never pay a broker's commission for shares purchased through a reinvestment plan. When you buy shares of stock, and you have used the experience and advice of your broker to help you decide which stock to buy, you pay a sales tax, and a commission to your broker. Commissions are the broker's salary and, in my opinion, a reliable and conscientious broker deserves every commission he or she earns. But once you are a stockholder in a company, there is no point in paying a fee to obtain additional shares if you don't have to do it.

Furthermore, commissions are higher on the purchase of an uneven number of shares, called an odd lot, than they are on the purchase of shares sold by a hundred, a round lot. For example, it would cost you more, in commissions, to buy twenty-five shares of stock at four different times, than to buy one hundred shares of the same stock but in one purchase. A reinvestment plan does not penalize an investor who has a few dollars to spend at any one time.

Another advantage is this: many companies sell their stock to reinvestment shareholders for a price that is lower than the one available to other buyers. If XYZ stock is selling for $20.00 a share and you can buy it for $19.50, why pass up the bargain?

DIVIDEND RECORDS

Company Name: _____

Year	Date	Amount	Date	Amount	Date	Amount	Date	Amount	Year Total

Reinvestment shares

All of these advantages outweigh the slight nuisance of some additional record keeping if the idea of a dividend reinvestment plan appeals to you.

But where is your dividend reinvestment stock? Where are the certificates that prove you own these new shares in the XYZ Company? Your broker doesn't have them in "street name" for you. They are not in your safe deposit box. The XYZ Company keeps this stock for you. Your printed proof of ownership is on the quarterly statements they send you. This is another example as to why you must keep these records!

There also is a very good reason for not joining a reinvestment plan. You could make an educated decision to buy stock in another company, but first you need to accumulate some of your surplus income for the purchase. In order to carry out this plan, you will deposit the dividend checks you receive from the XYZ Company, add any other surplus cash you have, and eventually return to your broker with sufficient funds for a new stock purchase.

No matter what investment decision you make for your surplus income, whether you choose a mutual fund or individual stocks, and no matter what choice you make for the use of your dividend income from your investments, you can be absolutely confident about one thing: you are not going to become wealthy in a few years! All of the "get rich quick" plans also carry a guarantee: you can become poor in a hurry. Given these alternatives, I am willing to keep my investment vehicles in the slower lane.

Expert advice

What does an expert say about investing? (So far, you have had only my words, the non-expert opinion.) I don't know how you react when you see an author include a long quote from someone else, but I always assume it's there because the author cannot say it. In this instance, that is absolutely true. I don't give investment advice, and Richard Russell does. Furthermore, I think he says it well and, naturally, I agree with him or I would not like his advice.

July 29, 1981. Dow Theory Letters 814, page 4, by Richard Russell.

"THOUGHTS: I receive dozens of letters and phone calls every week from investors, stock traders, commodity traders, amateur crap-shooters, fund managers, corporate officers, you name it. Many of these people have problems with their personal investments, and the number and depth of these problems often causes me to shake my head in sympathy and disbelief.

But one good thing comes out of all these letters and calls, and it is that I have an opportunity to see where people go right, and where they go wrong in their money and market operations. Following are a few of my thoughts.

(1) The average person really has little grasp of the basic principles of capital accumulation. In other words, he doesn't know how to make money. The person has some vague idea of buying this or jumping in and out there or grabbing some stock that his broker promised him "will double." But there's no overall plan, there's no consideration of risk/reward, there's no understanding of the why's and how's of handling money. As a result the average individual's record is a hodge-podge of good and (mostly) bad moves, the net result being a highly unsatisfactory performance.

(2) I was recently asked to discuss the best piece of investment advice that I, personally, had ever received. Here it is: it was given by the retiring financial editor of the old *New York Herald Tribune*. The editor stated that most young people make a basic financial mistake. They marry, and immediately they go into heavy debt by buying a house, a car, a washer-dryer and all the other "necessary" paraphernalia. This is exactly OPPOSITE to what they should do, he said. The editor then stated that the young people have TIME on their side. Therefore, instead of going into debt they should SAVE and allow their savings to work for them by COMPOUNDING through time. In this way, they can build a fortune during the 30 or 40 years that lie ahead of them. But going into debt early, said the editor, almost always means staying in debt while using your available incomes simply to pay off creditors. Debt makes you a slave while saving and assets make you the master of your financial fate. This was the BEST advice I've ever received anywhere. I thoroughly believed it at the time, and I have always operated on this basis. Consequently, I have never built up any debt, and I never owed anyone anything."

Don't you think he gives us a well-stated opinion? Remember . . . this is an opinion, not a truth. It is advice from, in this instance, two experts.

It's up to you!

I cannot stress one point strongly enough, and that's why I keep repeating it and saying it in different ways: you, and only you, know what to do with your money. Yes, ask for advice. Certainly, use your experts from your support team. But *please* — make all your own decisions.

Occasionally I feel a lack of confidence. I think to myself, "Maybe I should let my broker decide for me. She has studied investing. He does this all day. This is his or her business.

Well, I have studied, too. I read. I listen. If that person is so smart, then why is he still working to make a living? I can decide what is best for me. After all, it's my money!"

Finally, as we finish this chapter on the organization of investments, I want to take you back to the first chapter in the book for one reminder.

When I promised you cash from chaos, I took care to inform you that you could not get to the cash without practical, hard work and effort. Furthermore, I guaranteed you a return of *peace of mind* from an investment of time and energy spent on getting organized.

Risky business

Unfortunately, financial investments do not carry promises and guarantees. You never will have a care-free *or* worry-free system for investing. If you do, you probably are doing something wrong. It is important for you, and for your family, to be very honest with yourself and your investment advisors as to how much risk you can tolerate — both emotionally and financially. And you must be willing to continue your self education for as long a time as you are in control of your personal finances.

That's a rather somber ending to a subject as exciting as investments. There is another side to this. You could find, as I did many years ago, you have a wonderful time with investing; that it is a fascinating and rewarding experience — both financially and emotionally. I hope that is your discovery too.

One last word on investing . . . a conversation I had with a recent college graduate seated next to me on an airplane.

"My Dad's a stockbroker. He wants me to come into his company and learn the business."

"Aren't you lucky! That's a great opportunity."

"I'm not sure," he said, "I think working with investments all day could be pretty boring."

Boring? I couldn't let his comment go by.

"It's the only business I know where you learn everything that's going on in the entire world. The stock market is the national debt and a late freeze in Florida. It's whether China controls Hong Kong. Who gets elected President — or prime minister or premier. Pac Man, petroleum, peace or war."

He has a chance to continue his education. I hope he takes it.

8.

The Buddy System

In the early part of the book, I told you to give a copy of your written and photo inventory to your buddy. Who is this mysterious person?

Your significant other

It is a somebody else in your life — a trusted relative or friend — who does *not* live with you. An inventory kept in your own shelter would not be of much help if you ever should have a devastating fire. When you up-date your own inventory each new year, be sure to revise your buddy's copy also.

On being single

You can have more than one buddy. In fact, you must have a somebody else who will know all about your record keeping system. Why? Let's use an example. Her name is Martha and she lives alone.

Martha began the system several years ago and she now has a row of annual files on the floor of a closet. Her notebook, checkbook and accordion file are all up to date. Her investment folders are in a desk drawer. So far, no problem. However . . .

One night, as Martha drives home alone from a movie, a speeding car hits hers. She is taken to the hospital and remains unconscious for quite some time. Her only relative, a son, lives in another state.

Fortunately, a few years ago Martha had explained to him all about her system. She had shown him where her records were and how she kept her files. Since her son is a co-owner of her safe deposit box, he can remove her auto and medical insurance policies to review her coverage and protection clauses. He knows all about his mother's personal finances and can take care of everything for her until she returns home.

Sharing

What if you do not live alone? Explain your system to another member of your household. Roommates should share a mutual responsibility for each other. As a married couple, both husband and wife must be familiar with every phase of their joint personal finances. There are hundreds of true stories in which the surviving spouse (usually the wife) knows absolutely nothing about the financial affairs of the deceased. Keys to safe deposit boxes are found in desk drawers and the location and contents of these boxes remains a mystery.

The children's hour

I want to take the buddy system a step further. Parents have a responsibility to explain the financial organization system to somebody else as long as their children are too young to understand it.

However, once the children in a family reach high school age, the parents should teach them the system. Not only are you protecting your children from an additional stress should there be an emergency involving both parents, you are teaching *them* to be money managers.

Here is a personal example. When my daughter began high school, I sat down with her and we went through all my current records, as if I were teaching her the system. I showed her where all my duplicate keys were. I asked her to go through an annual file and tell me if there was anything she didn't understand. Then I invited her to go out to lunch with me one day soon.

We had our lunch and went to my bank so she could meet some of the people who worked there. We stopped at the offices of my lawyer, broker, and CPA so she could meet the other members of my support team. Naturally I had phoned each one in advance of this day and explained my purpose in stopping by.

Many things were accomplished in that one day. She was proud of my confidence and trust in her. She learned more about the businesses of each of these professionals. I was assured she would not have to talk to total strangers if there were ever a family tragedy. She furthered her own education in money and finance in a realistic way. We also had a great lunch and lots of fun together.

Senior citizens

The buddy system can function in yet another relationship. Are you the one person who is responsible for a parent, older relative, or friend? Spend a few hours with that person and explain the need for written records — especially in the event of illness or death.

This is not a tactless nor intrusive action. On the contrary, it is tangible evidence that you care about this person. By being a buddy, you give peace of mind to somebody else.

I am the one person responsible for my elderly parents. I have shown them my notebook, particularly the first section (support team), and explained the importance of these records. Together, we made a similar written record of their permanent and vital information. I keep a copy of this data in my accordion file pocket labeled "Personal."

When I first set up the system, I gave myself a test. I suggest you take the same test and answer it for your particular situation. "If I die next Tuesday, who is the one somebody in my life who can, in ten minutes, know everything about my personal finances?" Once you decide on that person, be sure you explain the information.

A happy ending

As I organize my life, I make every effort to organize my death. I will not avoid planning my dying. I don't know anyone who is three hundred years old, or who has lived forever. I suspect I will not be the first.

The way I see it, I don't expect somebody else to plan my parties or vacations. Why should I expect another person to plan my death?

Besides, once you have it planned, you don't have to worry about it. One more worry to avoid.

Without a lot of things to worry about, I have time for

foolishness. I want to show you some numbers. They are not important — this exercise is just for fun.

The computer game

Since I am interested in personal financial organization, I took a computer course with the idea of buying a home computer. At the completion of the course, I shopped for and priced an *electronic* system that could replace my old notebook and files. I wanted to know my return before I made the investment.

I looked into two costs: time and money. The return I demand is flexibility, simplicity, and a non-limiting system. I don't have all the exact numbers but here is what I found out:

Your System

Time: per week — 20 minutes

Equipment: closet floor, desk drawer

Utility cost: one light bulb

Service: 1 package notebook paper

Information load: no limit

Cost:

check file	$ 1.50
accordion file	$ 7.00
annual file	$ 2.15
notebook	$ 3.00
paper	$ 1.65
dividers	$ 1.65
Investment folders (4)	$ 1.00 each
Investments records page (4)	$ .04 each
Total:	$21.11 not incl. tax

Electronic System
(Cheapest computer I could find)

Time: per week — tape new information, add to program, hook up to TV, transcribe into checkbook

Equipment: cables, plugs, dust cover, work table for components

Utility cost: TV, computer, cassette recorder and one light bulb

Service: repairs and adjustments, phone first, Mon-Fri, 9-5 if not busy

Information load: 26 limited categories

Cost:

cassette recorder	$ 60.00
computer	$300.00
Total:	$360.00 not incl. tax

Obviously I have not tried to be specific, although the cost figures are real numbers. I had a fine time making this comparison. I have not even mentioned "good" home computers cost many hundreds or thousands of dollars.

I went to a dinner party the other evening. The host invited us to come into his information center (it used to be a den) and look at his computer set-up. I smile every time I imagine inviting people to look in my closet and see my "programmed and stored" information.

Can you put a computer under your arm and take it to an IRS audit? Can you sit by the fire, or outside on the patio, to enter your computer records? Will a power failure affect your file or your notebook?

Yes, I have made another choice based on my study of the information and my needs. I may have a computer someday. For now, my system is easier, faster, and a whole lot cheaper.

Speaking of information . . .

Knowing right from wrong

I have read a great number of books and articles on financial organization and I continuously study, not just read, newspapers, books, and magazines on finance and money. There is excellent information in some of these materials, and there is wrong and foolish information in many of them. Sort it out — the good from the bad — and use what is best for you.

I am sure you have noticed an absence of graphs, tables and statistics in this book. I did not include them because I think most people find them boring and won't read them anyway. Also, any numbers I could write now will be out of date by the time you read them.

A perpetual student

One piece of information will not change. Everytime you do anything with your money, find out all the available information *before* you make a decision. That must seem so obvious to you, you wonder why I bother to say it. Do you remember when money market funds were paying 16% interest? I know many people who continued to deposit their money in passbook savings accounts and receive 5½% interest. They ignored the changes that were taking place in our economy.

There is not now, and there never will be, one best way to take care of your money and investments. You will never finish your class. Your money always will be affected by new laws, interest rates, bank programs, and the new electronics.

Could it be that someday we won't have any money? Maybe each of us will have a master code card to use for everything we buy — even time on a parking meter. Until that day arrives, I urge you —

Keep your records.

Read and listen.

Ask questions.

Be flexible.

Make your own decisions.

And find some free paper clips!

Review

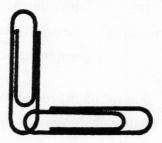

The following outline of the basic steps in financial organization is included as a handy reference guide. You may find it helpful to remove the guide and keep it on your desk until you are completely familiar with all the phases of your record keeping system.

ORGANIZATION GUIDE

ONCE A WEEK

1. Pay bills by date due. Include identifying numbers and facts on checks, stubs and receipts.

2. Enter all information in notebook. ✔ on stubs.

3. Balance check book. Include all "D's" on stubs.

4. Staple deposit receipts to stubs.

5. File "pieces of paper" in accordion file.

6. Enter information in investment folders.

ONCE A MONTH

1. Reconcile bank statement with checkbook.

2. Circle (o) or check (✔) on stub numbers.

3. File statement and cancelled checks (5 x 11 file).

ONCE A YEAR

1. Make annual file.

2. Complete charts.

3. File warranties and guarantees.

4. Update inventory, safe deposit box.

5. Notebook: update permanent pages, total old pages, add new pages.

6. Inform "buddy" of any revisions.

7. Review goals and accomplishments.

End Note

The organization of personal finances — the system described in this book — is the product of many generous benefactors. Some of them are the men and women who attend my classes and then modify my ideas to meet their needs. Some are clients who take the basic system and expand it to serve their complex financial situations. Others are the people who read my manuscript while it was in progress and offered me the benefits of their wisdom and experience in money management.

Always, it seems, there is someone who finds a better way to solve a problem. If you are one of the problem solvers, and if you would be willing to share your solutions with others, please send your ideas to:

> Jean Ross Peterson
> 1259 El Camino
> Suite 221
> Menlo Park, California 94025

I shall appreciate hearing from you and incorporating your suggestions into future editions of the system. The route that takes us out of chaos and leads us into cash is bumpy and filled with obstacles. If you can smooth the way and ease the transition, you will have the gratitude of many. Surely, you will have mine! Thank you.

Index